STAND EVEN

Copyright © 2016 by Kim Standeven

All rights reserved. No part of this publication may be reproduced, distributed, or transmitted in any form or by any means, including photocopying, recording, or other electronic or mechanical methods, without the prior written permission of the author, except in the case of brief quotations embodied in critical reviews and certain other noncommercial uses permitted by copyright law.

Printed and bound in Canada at McNally Robinson Booksellers.
1120 Grant Avenue, Winnipeg, Manitoba R3M 2A6.

Cover and Book design by McNally Robinson Booksellers.
Cover Image by Freepik

www.mcnallyrobinson.com/selfpublishing

First Edition

ISBN 978-1-77280-059-3

STAND EVEN

A mentorship memoir.
A mentorship philosophy.

KIM STANDEVEN

This book explores the power of mentorship by looking within first.

It describes how one defining experience brought me to my knees and taught me what my purpose is, and what it meant to stand back up and simply *be*.

"There is no greater agony than bearing an untold story inside you." —Maya Angelou[1]

To Mom—my mentor in determination

TABLE OF CONTENTS

Foreword 13
Introduction 17

PART ONE: WHY AWARENESS MATTERS

1 | The Ripple Effect 23
2 | Share Yourself 28

PART TWO: OUR JOURNEY TO STAND EVEN

3 | Ed, My Dad 39
4 | 3 AM 52
5 | Dig Deeper 59
6 | Legacy 72

PART THREE: MY AWAKENING

7 | The Bee Sting 77
8 | Letting Go 82
9 | Huh? 94

PART FOUR: THE LESSON APPLIES EVERYWHERE

10 | Hold up Your Mirror 101
11 | Check Yourself 112
12 | Be Inspired 119

Pictures 123
Afterword—Take Action and Share Yourself 125
Do Better—Journal Activity 127
Mentorship Model—A Look Within 136
Acknowledgements 139
Endnotes 141
About the Author 143

Foreword

When Kim told me she was writing a book about mentoring and her experiences in life, I was very interested and excited. I have worked closely with Kim as her mentor and teacher since 2012. I have a great interest in the world of coaching having co-designed the Coaching Program for Royal Roads University in Victoria, B.C. and then creating the Core Alignment Professional Coach Training Program at the Banff Leadership Centre. These courses have graduated many very successful business and personal coaches, Kim being among them.

There is a uniqueness in the way that Kim maintains "presence" when you are around her. She explains it as a gift, resulting from a specific physical handicap, which she shares in the book. Her ability to be authentically curious and to listen to you at a profound level makes her one of the best facilitators and coaches I know.

In Kim's book, *Stand Even*, she has opened us up to aspects of mentorship that are available to everyone. As Kim asks, "What is mentorship?", she shows us the value in taking an honest and open-minded look at what our experiences might provide for us already. If one continues to walk through life as a student, learner, and as someone who intends to contribute to the greater good, these lessons are invaluable, as long as we're listening for them.

From day one of the Core Alignment Coaching course, I could see that Kim was going to be one of those who would impact many people in the world. She committed herself to become increasingly vulnerable and present. After graduating as a professional coach, Kim apprenticed and became a facilitator of the "Authentic To The Core" retreat. This workshop-retreat has been a stand-alone Personal and Professional Development Program for the last twenty years, and she hosts it beautifully.

There is a saying about "the student becoming master to the teacher," or in this case, the mentor allows herself to be mentored by the student. I am honoured to have been and to continue to be one of Kim's mentors.

The book will touch the hearts of many, helping them to see and experience a different perspective to mentoring and mentorship. In reading it, I have reflected on my own life.

Growing up in a large family of mixed French/Indigenous heritage, it seemed natural for me to gravitate to those I considered as mentors. Each of us children had different interests and concerns, and there were enough aunts and uncles, grandparents, and friends around for us to access the mentorship we sought. We naturally allowed nature to mentor us. By engaging with the lakes, rivers, and streams, we learned not only to trust but to respect their power and gentleness—things that we would carry into our lives.

The three main themes or principles in this book apply to all areas of our lives. *Take the time.* For me this has been and continues to be a guiding principle that I do well with at times—and other times not so much, so the book serves as a type of mentor too. Three years ago, I decided to "take the time" in my life by intentionally creating a slower life purpose. I cut out the business travel that was such a huge part of my life and reduced my work week to four days. This has been the best thing I have done at this stage of my life. It is allowing me to take the time for me, for my family, and sometimes for just doing nothing.

It is nice to be seen. I had my 10-year-old grandson with me this one particular weekend. He was so helpful and respectful, and even a bit of a gentleman. I reflected on the book and acknowledged each thing he did, making sure he knew how much I appreciated it. At the end of the weekend he said, "Thank you very much, Ama, for all the compliments. I like it when you notice stuff."

Lastly, *When it matters say something.* As it was for Kim, one of the greatest informal mentors in my life was my father. From a very early age he taught me the need and value of speaking up when something was important, whether it was about family matters, school issues, or career concerns. I probably lean towards the "outer edge" of speaking up when it matters, and at times it can get me into trouble. Yet I would much rather lean that way than the alternative way of being quiet and careful.

I hope you enjoy all of the great lessons, philosophies, and practices that Kim offers in this very intimate and rich story. It will continue to be a resource for me when I need reminders of how to live an authentic, high-quality life, and how to Stand Even!

Warmest,

Lori-Anne Demers MCC

Master Certified Coach
Author of *Authentic To The Core.*
www.demersgroup.com

Introduction

"I wish I could live a little more.
Look up to the sky, not just the floor."—Adele[2]

The first time I heard Adele soulfully sing these two lines, tears welled in my eyes. I had been searching for the right language to describe the purpose of writing this book, the purpose for sharing my soul with the world. Nothing felt quite right—until I heard these words. Yes, these seventeen words are the anchor for everything I do in my life. That's because for much of my existence, all I did was look down at the floor. No longer!

This is a book about being aware. To notice how you are presenting yourself and to live life awake rather than on autopilot. I strive to live a life where I spend more time looking up at the sky and feeling free rather than looking at my feet and feeling weighed down. My hope for myself—and for you—is to learn from all of it, whether we are looking down or looking up. To find the gift in all of our experiences and work toward living with our heads up, fully present, standing proud and even.

Simply put, this is a memoir containing some elements of a self-help book. When I first starting writing, I discovered

I was actually helping myself as I wrote. I felt better. I felt free from the accumulated years of experiences that felt like bags of rocks hanging from my shoulders. It dawned on me that perhaps if I shared my story it might actually help others. So here I am, a person who had always identified myself as being deep, proud when people called me an old soul, a typical wife, and mother of two. But I had never considered myself as a writer who would publish a book with the intention of inspiring others to see life's experiences in a new light and to define what mentorship means in their own lives. Yet the writer in me blossomed. Yes, I wrote a memoir, but it is also a self-help book. I truly hope it helps.

What will this book help you with? This book is about defining mentorship and discovering how it shows up in our lives. It is about how powerful mentorship is if we are willing to explore ourselves. Our greatest mentors can be found in our experiences and the people with whom we interact every day. My invitation to you as you read my story is to allow for a shift in your own perceptions and beliefs. To be open to the possibility that your experiences are a great gift waiting to be explored and to be open to a definition of mentorship you may have never considered before. My invitation is for you to open the door to your own wisdom through reading about the opening of my door. Will you be moved by my story? I cannot answer that, but I hope it stirs something in you to look a little deeper at the people and experiences that make up your past and present. Just maybe it will influence who you invite into your future and the life you decide to create going forward. Just maybe it will influence who you choose to be—how you choose to behave—at work and at home. Just maybe you will walk away with more questions and some answers about what you stand for.

Each chapter offers a glimpse into what mentorship means for me and how it shows up for me as a working woman, a daughter, a mother, and a person who finally accepted the deepest, most raw feelings of her heart and decided to take a leap of faith to share them openly. I ask questions, share stories, and offer an invitation for you to pick up the tools you may need so you can move forward in your own life. What I am offering is a door. It will be up to you to open it and up to you to decide what to do with what you find on the other side of that door—what to reflect on and how to choose how you want to present yourself in your professional and personal life. The purpose is to enhance the relationships you have with your experiences, your peers, and your loved ones. Will you experience an expanded point of view? I truly hope so.

As I've said, this book is part memoir and part self-help book. I had an experience with someone who ended up being a powerful mentor without realizing it at the time. I am peeling back the layers of this experience that first brought me to my knees, then pushed me on my journey to stand back up and choose who I wanted to be.

It all started when I was fourteen years old in the kitchen with my dad. That was the moment the door began to open …

Part One

Why Awareness Matters

Chapter One

The Ripple Effect

"Kim, why are you doing that?" my mom inquires.

"What am I doing?" I ask, confused.

I am in my early twenties enjoying a visit home with Mom. I am siting on the couch, holding my hands in front of me, my fingers intertwined as though I'm holding a boyfriend's hand as we walk. I am rolling my thumbs round and round each other, over and over. I don't even realize I'm doing it. It is soothing and meditative, I guess.

"Mum-mum used to do that all the time. She would sit and roll her thumbs," she said.

I don't remember my great-grandmother, whom I know only from pictures. *Hmm*, I think, *how interesting. I wonder what else has been passed on?* Over the years, this seemingly insignificant observation has stuck with me. Now that I have my own family I am more curious about my ancestors and their impact. *I wonder what my impact will be?*

Today, as I sit in the present moments I am often taken away into the world of wondering. In my mind and in my heart, I imagine the future generations of my family, their faces, their laughter, and their pain. I wonder what parts of me may one day show up in them. I believe we are all connected, and although I cannot explain it or even put it into words, my inner knowing tells me that who I choose to be is bigger than just me. Challenging ourselves to learn and grow is such a great gift. Growth is the recipe for a rich and fulfilling life and the ripple effect of our efforts are beyond our comprehension.

These days, I am continually asking myself what is possible for our children, our children's children, and for the generations we cannot even picture but know are around the corner. How will my perspective and willingness to grow influence them? How will our connections and our lessons and how we present ourselves to the world show up down the line, I wonder?

This book feels bigger than just writing about my story. It feels as if I am putting into motion something bigger than myself. Above all, I have a *knowing* that our lives mean something, so I want to honour our mentors for the lessons with which they gift us. I want to gift others with a new perspective and perhaps a chance to learn from as many amazing people as possible. If each individual stretches themselves to live to their full potential, to use their experiences in a positive way, future generations will benefit from that investment. What if our lives and this universe of eternal energy are like a bank account? I don't want to bounce any future cheques because I wasn't willing to invest my stories.

In my own home, I walk down the long hallway in my basement for a jar of spaghetti sauce—but then I stop. The cement floor is cold on my feet, yet my heart fills with warmth as I look at the wall of family pictures—our family tree. Their eyes follow me, and their images enchant me as if they are reaching out of the photo to tap me on the shoulder. These are the faces of my immediate family, my grandparents, and my great-grandparents. Their pictures connect me to the generations before them, reminding me that their lives mattered. Their stories mattered. My mind slows and I take a moment to silently express my gratitude.

Thank you for your resilience and courage, I think as I reflect on the hardships they endured and the successes they created. I think about my great-grandfather, who, as a teenager, stowed away on a ship from Bulgaria. I think about my great-grandmother, who endured unimaginable poverty while raising twelve children.

They have become the guiding lights on my path, and now it is my turn to light the way for those who may one day stop and stare into the eyes of my photo. I am not exactly sure what stopped me from picking up that homemade jar of spaghetti sauce from the storage room, but it had something to do with Great-Grandma Van grabbing my attention. Our family calls her Annie V and I feel grateful that I was able to get to know one of my great grandparents. I am transported back to her little two-room house. She was a four-foot-nothing, redheaded Scottish woman who relentlessly held on to her fighting spirit. The image I recall of her crooked arthritic hands reminds me of all she endured. She was feisty and fierce. A survivor. Her house was cozy, warm, and smelled of soup. We would sit at the white retro kitchen table, one that might belong in a fifties diner. We would play rummy and banter about the rules of the game, which seemed to change with every card played. She would get up to offer me a mint that she had cut into quarters to save a penny or two. "Mint?" she asked.

Oh, Annie V, how I miss your spunk and wisdom. I return from that moment of reverie, grab my spaghetti sauce, and continue making supper for my own family, grateful for the blessed life I have and the incredible people who made it possible that I was ever born. That supper never tasted so good!

This is my story. However, what I really care about are the amazing lessons *you* hold close to your heart. I care about who stops you in your tracks when you think of them. My hope is that my story resonates with you and inspires you to reflect on your everyday mentors and the things you learn from them—often subconsciously. I hope that, as you read my words, they spark something in you—to wonder, to become curious about what mentorship means to you. Perhaps right now, while someone is mentoring you, you are having an impact on someone else—mentoring them. I believe that we can all change how we see the world by sharing about the people who touch our souls. By sharing our learning and what is important to us, we have an opportunity to change how future generations interact. We can create a lasting legacy, a ripple effect beyond our imagination.

It starts with each of us cultivating a willingness to begin sharing. I am reminded of my great-grandparents' and grandparents' generations, when a great stigma about sharing existed. They rarely talked about their experiences, especially the ones that were deemed taboo. They didn't talk of their hardships, but were expected to suck it up. Family secrets and hiding in the shadows seemed to be the norm. I want to honour all of the untold stories and life lessons, some of which died along with them. I wonder if the essence of those lessons and traits somehow shows up unexpectedly, like the twirling of my thumbs. I wonder about my willingness to voice my learning and intentionally engage in the act of sharing my most powerful experiences—*will this catapult our family's evolution in some way?* I wonder … hmm.

My feelings about sharing my experiences intensified after I gave birth to my second daughter. I'd always had a desire to write a book "one day," and it occurred to me that the "one day" should be today. I no longer wanted to take for granted that tomorrow would come—I have no control over tomorrow. So I started to write while the kids were sleeping. An hour here and there. The words flowed. I wrote ideas on scraps of paper, waiting for those moments when I could sit and explore them. The one thing my journey in life has taught me is that I cannot guarantee my tomorrows, so if I want to do something that matters, I had better do it right now. I decided to stop denying the part of me that wanted to share. By saying yes, it opened me up to so much more than I ever thought could be there. I don't want to risk that my life experiences, my lessons, and legacy might end with me, so I am preserving them in this book as a representation of who I am right now. I will not let the wisdom of this journey disappear. My story is important. Our story is important. Your story is important.

As I looked into the eyes on our "family history wall," I wished I knew more about their lives, their passions, and what mattered to them. I imagine this book like a stone being dropped into the middle of a smooth lake, a perfect glass-like surface. The subtle ripples start to move toward the shore. One after the other, after the other, again and again and again. I imagine that my story brings up memories of stories in others, and the ripples, like ocean waves, once they begin, they never stop. The energy is infinite and the impact is felt for generations to come. This book is about being known and sharing our stories.

Chapter Two

Share Yourself

The lessons we learn while living our lives and being in contact with various mentors help us discern the values that we will hold close to our hearts. These values shape how we behave in all facets of our life, whether in personal relationships or at work. In order to learn *being*, we need to experience with all of our senses. In my experience, the only way to truly undergo transformational learning is to experience it at a visceral level. Our experiences have a purpose. They reveal to us what matters and give us a glimpse to who we are at our core.

    I learned so much from the journey I am about to share. Why did I learn so much? I believe it is because of the depth of my feelings on my way through that journey. It amazes me how a memory can be so vivid and that we can relive it with such intensity. Like hearing a song on the radio from our teenage days and how it takes us right back there, as if we had been teleported through time. The colours, smells, and emotions—all of it. These intense experiences are where profound learning can be uncovered. A memory is very powerful and can keep us stuck unless we change our relationship with it. That is my hope for you—not to be stuck as long as I was. When I relive a moment, I accept it as part of who I am—but it doesn't rule my present. There is a space between my past and my present, much like the subtle silence between musical notes, which allows me a sense of peace. Our experiences, whether joyful or painful, are meant to help us grow. While not keeping us stuck in the past, they do reflect back to us what we stand for, what matters to us.

I still remember the hurt in my mother's eyes when one day, though I tried to say it under my breath, she heard me calling her a bitch. My teenage rage had gotten the better of me. I was frustrated with my life at the time, constantly bottling up my anger. When I could no longer contain it, for no reason at all I ended up directing it at her. She just stared at me, shell-shocked, then turned and walked away. I am sure it was because she didn't want me to see her cry.

As I think back about the incident, though I didn't notice whether she had cried, I feel her pain. My mom never swore. Respect is important to her, and I know I had violated her. I learned about the power of one's words and the effect they can have on another human being, who in this case happened to be my mother. I wrote her a letter of apology, telling her how sorry I was. The hurt in her eyes taught me a valuable lesson. To this day, I am very aware of the power of words and especially aware of when I feel an urge to strike out at someone or something by name-calling. I often now find myself taking a breath before I speak—I never again want to hurt another person in that way. It is important to me to remember that I cannot take words back. Ever. They cut deep. I will never forget what I saw in Mom's eyes.

What strikes me about this experience is that I don't remember what I was mad about. It might have been about cleaning my room or doing the dishes, I have no idea. What

I do remember was who I was *being* in that moment and how it felt. This is one of my first vivid visceral memories of not living aligned with my values. I know this because it tugged on my heart until I made amends by writing her a letter. This is an important point because people are going to remember how it felt to be around you, even if they have forgotten what you were doing in the moment. This is why learning and having conversations about *being* is crucial to our growth. *Doing* comes and goes, but *being* is the constant that holds us up and keeps us standing even.

When I reflect on my deeply felt experiences, I can list many beautiful, joyful memories that bring tears of laughter and feelings of warmth. For example, the spark I felt when I met my husband for the first time and knew he was going to be a constant in my life. The moments of wonder, laughter, and tears are the visceral response that lead to great personal discoveries. I believe I am not able to grow and expand my thinking without being willing to feel fully. There are mentors all around us, making a huge difference in our lives, even if they are unaware that they are mentoring. I believe we can change the world by sharing our stories and our most visceral memories and experiences we have received because of these mentors.

Take a moment right now and do a little exercise for yourself by answering a couple of questions:

Who do you know who has provided you with some valuable lessons you would want to pass on to others?

Why is that person important to you, and why are the lessons important?

Examining those questions became part of my life's roadmap and why I started writing this book.

Did I have any other influences? To answer that, I have to go back to my school days. Even back then, I had always had the desire to share my thoughts but was afraid of being judged, or even worse, laughed at. I can remember an experience I had when I was in Grade 5. I am standing at the front of the class, knees wobbling and voice shaking. I felt very grown up behind that classroom podium. *This is what it must feel like to be an adult*, I think. It is my first speech, and I share my heart openly about what I want to do when I grow up. There is that "do" part again!

"Mr. Johnson, fellow classmates. Hello, my name is Kim, and when I grow up I want to be a teacher." I tell everyone that I don't want to be just any teacher, but one that helps kids who have special needs. I proudly tell the kids this and they clap. Afterwards, on the playground, I find out what they really think. The clapping was a courtesy. A couple of the kids point and laugh, teasing me about my dream to help others.

"Hey, Kim. Only retards hang out with retards!"

As my heart sinks, I decide that it is dangerous to share my heart so openly. From then on, I keep things to myself. I close my heart to protect it from being a further target. This is my first memory of building walls. Over the years, as they became higher and higher, my voice became quieter and quieter.

As I reflect on that time in my life, I am still amazed at how quickly my voice became silenced. Back then, I was so desperate to fit in that I decided to fit in by disappearing. How many of us can relate to the feeling of being laughed at or the feeling of being an outsider? A lot of us, I'll bet. Until I started writing, I didn't realize just how long my voice had been lost to me. That whole classroom experience started me on a path of people pleasing, because like most folks, I desperately wanted to be liked. I stayed in unhealthy relationships, put up with people, and kept my mouth shut in order to be liked and accepted. This trend followed me throughout my school years, into my career, and into my personal life.

At the age of thirty-three, I experienced an awakening. I found my voice again and am now ready to stand tall. I am reminded every single day about standing tall since it is in my name—Standeven. I am often asked whether Standeven is really my name. Yes, it is. It is on my birth certificate. I did not make it up for the purpose of this book. It is my name, and I share it with many others whom I assume are as proud of it as I am. Was "stand even" to be part of my destiny as I use my name to symbolize whom I choose to be? Is it an anchor for my own legacy as I move through my experiences? It is definitely a powerful reminder of who I am and how I choose to present myself in this life. Although I didn't become the schoolteacher I had envisioned as a young child, I have become more than I ever could have imagined. I identify with the labels of teacher and healer, and this book and my work as a life coach is a testament to that. If I had the opportunity to redo that Grade 5 speech, I would tell everyone that when I grew up I wanted to be a person who helped others "stand even." A teacher who stood for being courageous, open minded, and inspiring. I would tell them that was the teacher I would strive to be, and I am now on the path.

I cannot explain why, but I have a fire inside, compelling me to share my story. Do I still have some of those earlier fears about acceptance? Sure I do. The fear creeps into my mind, and it often says things to me such as, "Who do you think you are, Kim?" and "Why would anyone care about what you have to say?" The voice in my head is harsh, like that of a bully, but I am willing to fight back now and stand up tall. I can now face my inner bully and say, "Take a hike!"

I ask myself, "What is the big picture here?" and my response is always similar. It is about remembering the place in my early history where I built those protective walls around me and how I eventually learned to knock them down. It is about inspiring others and being a leader. It is about living my dreams and showing my children how to push past the critiquing bully that lives in their own heads.

After having lived this part of my journey and having experienced the world thus far, I realize that many of us feel the same things—fears, rejection, and not feeling good enough. If we were to share ourselves occasionally, we might not feel so alone or on the outside. How do I know this? Because I know so many who tell me of their fears. My career is all about giving people a safe place in which to share their fears and then offering the support they need in order to move through it all. We cannot wait forever to conquer our fears and begin to share ourselves. Yes, there may be those who will laugh or try to tear us down like the kids did to me in my Grade 5 class. I also know there will be more who will choose to embrace and love, and that is what makes it worth any risk. I merely take a deep breath and tell myself to "share yourself."

I know my purpose is to collaborate with others as they explore their own inner knowing in an effort to become aware of who they want to be. The learning and the questions we need to ask ourselves are as unique as our fingerprints, and yet it sometimes takes a guide, someone who will help us notice that uniqueness. It is time to chip away at the walls that surround our hearts. The fears we may be feeling are not based in reality. Once I became aware of this, it made it easier for me to stand up for myself and move forward. So I say we need to share our hearts. The world needs all of us to be true to ourselves, to take risks, and to push out of our comfort zones. What if my desire for something more in my life was greater than my fears? I looked at that question and knew the answer—and knew I had found my reason to write. I had never written anything in my life other than a periodic journal entry and school essay—but the energy to write was always there, under the surface, waiting until I was ready to tap into it.

I had a strong desire, and I decided to focus on it rather than on any fears that tried to creep in and suppress it. As that strong desire began to surface, I decided to nurture it. The fear loosened its grip on me. I realized that desire trumps fear every time. I let desire be the spark in my life. I had a choice. Would I focus on building a big beautiful fire created by that spark or would I let fear suck the oxygen from my fire? I decided to choose the fire, and "share yourself" became my desire, my mantra, the fire I chose to stoke. I was tired of living life without a voice, so I took it back from the fear that had stolen it and said, "Fear, take a hike!"

This brings me to the everyday people. They are the ones who have made the biggest impact in my life. These are the mentors who live among us, not labelling themselves as mentors, but rather just living a life that matters to them and being the best of themselves. I could probably write pages and pages about important people who have taught me valuable lessons in my life. I'll bet you could as well, if you gave it some thought.

In this book, I am choosing to focus on one person in particular. The learning from our journey together was profound on so many levels. That person's name is Ed and he is my father. I should also add that he has passed on, no longer with me in body but with me nonetheless.

From my dad, I learned mentorship as well as the importance of legacy. I am constantly asking myself, "How do I want to be remembered? What are the characteristics I want to be known for?" It isn't about living my life for other people or their agendas. It is about making decisions based on the type of person I want to be for myself and for them. There is a subtle but very important distinction there. Let's take a look at that distinction as I introduce you to my father.

I want to honour and share a glimpse of who my dad was. I want to share with you the lessons he passed on to me in the hope that they will ignite a spark of your own. I believe the more deeply we share, the greater we become. I believe we can change and heal the world by sharing our stories, changing the conversations we have with ourselves and with others, one story at a time.

Part Two

Our Journey to Stand Even

Chapter Three

Ed, My Dad

He was standing by the fridge holding himself up on the kitchen counter. Something didn't seem right, and I didn't like the looks of it. It was an early morning in 1992, and Dad and I were in the kitchen. He was forty-two years old at the time, and I was fourteen. Dad was a blue-collar guy, a welder by trade, and a weekend biker who exuded strength. I was a proud daddy's girl who saw her dad as a strong badass. He was not a big guy, just five-foot-seven tops, but he had muscles, worked hard, and in my eyes was invincible. He had a cool presence, reminding me of the Fonz from *Happy Days*, a popular 1970s TV show,[3] and he was my hero.

I witnessed him break down only once—that time I cycled to his house with my brother when my parents were divorcing. It was a time when he let down his tough exterior, and in that moment I sensed we were heading down a similar path.

On this day, it happened to be our weekend with Dad. Seemingly another normal day but Dad was unusually quiet, his head down. I sensed something was wrong.

"Dad? What's wrong?"

He looked up. "Kim, I can't see."

"What do you mean, Dad?"

"When I was driving home last night, I had trouble keeping my truck from veering off the road. I was afraid I might hit someone. I thought I had the flu. I can't see. My eyes. I can't see."

There was fear in his voice. I became afraid too. I somehow knew this was about to turn out very badly for our family. I was filled with anxiety and dread, my mind a mess, and I now don't remember who we called or how he got to the hospital. I just remember that my brother and I weren't allowed to see him for quite some time. The doctors and nurses seemed frantic.

"Please have a seat in the waiting room. We'll give you an update once we've run some tests. It's okay—your dad is in good hands." The nurse gently suggests.

"Okay? He's going to be okay? How can you say that? Dad told me he couldn't see." I knew it wasn't all going to be okay. My brother and I waited and waited.

"Just go home, kids, " my grandmother and my dad's girlfriend said. "We'll phone as soon as we know what's happening. He's in good hands. It'll be okay."

So we went back to our mother's house, our home. The weekend with Dad was over.

A few hours later, my grandmother called. "They think he has a brain tumour. They're running more tests."

I was shattered. I was watching TV in the basement, trying to distract myself from all the "what ifs."

I hung up the phone and yelled, "Mom, Mom! It was Grandma. Mom, Mom!" I remember sobbing as I struggled up the stairs on all fours, knots in my stomach, frantic to get to my mother so she could take all the pain away. Climbing those stairs felt like climbing Mount Everest. Wondering about what was going to happen next was depleting all my oxygen. I started to hyperventilate. I couldn't breathe—all I could think about was that Dad couldn't see.

I remember a jumble of hospital visits, gowns, doctors, and family trying to keep things normal for us in what was a very abnormal situation. As it turned out, Dad didn't have a tumour, but there was internal bleeding in his brain. I buried all the fear, anger, despair, pain, hurt, and disappointment deep in my brain and body. I tucked it all away like a squirrel hiding nuts so nobody could find them, not even the squirrel. I didn't want anyone at school to notice anything out of the ordinary. I disappeared even further; I made myself fly under the radar, kept quiet, and put on a smile when I had to.

"I'm fine. There's nothing wrong. Just keep going," I kept telling myself. It all felt strange, as if I were outside myself, watching a movie of someone else's life.

Thinking back on that whole next year after Dad went into the hospital, I don't recall many specific memories of him. Our hospital visits felt like a TV rerun. The same conversations, the same place, the same people. It was the same each week. I became numb to it all and gradually shut out the world. During the two-hour car ride to the hospital most Sundays with my grandparents, I remember that numbness and sometimes a tingling feeling as I stared out the window.

Grandma and Grandpa tried to engage me. "How's school going, Kim?" or "Rainy day, eh?" I don't think they knew how to process it either. We all sat like statues, shells of ourselves. Mostly we sat in agonizing silence, never once discussing our fears or our pain. I felt frozen and built thicker walls around my heart. By age fifteen, those walls were well built and almost impenetrable.

Once he was stable enough, Dad and I took a walk. It was a nice break from the repetitive visits we had been experiencing. It was a cool, fall-like day, and I remember holding his hand as we shuffled along the hospital sidewalk. Hope seemed to hang in the air, and it felt good to wipe away the fears for a moment and dream about Dad coming home so we could play Yahtzee and take a ride on his Harley. We held hands, not only because he needed my physical support for his unsteady balance, but more so because Dad and I needed to connect as father and daughter, beyond the limitations of mere words. I remember feeling a bit awkward as I walked with him. I felt eyes probing as people passed by or stared from the safety of their cars, rubbernecking as though they had just seen a car accident. I am sure they wondered what our story was. Why was a young girl walking down the street with a man who limped and swayed at every step?

As for me, I was thinking, "Stop looking at me. I don't want to be noticed. We're living a nightmare here." Interesting how in that moment I wanted to escape back into the safety of the old rerun visits in the hospital room. I felt exposed and too vulnerable in the outside world. I wonder what Dad felt—he said nothing about what was happening with him. We just walked. I think he wanted to have things appear as normal as possible for my sake. I wished he would have said something, anything.

After a time, life once again began to feel as though it had some balance. Dad was released from the hospital and his driver's license was returned to him, so we felt a glimmer of hope. He even took a ten-hour bike trip up north on his beloved Harley. "I want to take a ride, just in case," he said. He must have sensed how fragile his situation was with all the unknowns about the current state of his health. Years later, my uncle shared with me that this ride was hard on Dad physically, but he did it because he was afraid he would never be able to ride again. Sadly, his vision of the future was all too accurate. Almost a year after his first attack, he was readmitted to the hospital. Tragically, for all of us, Dad relapsed. Some blood vessels in his brain had burst and the internal bleeding again became very serious.

I remember two crucial things about that time. First, how fragile he was. They told us there might be times when he thought he might be able to stand up or walk when, in fact, he could not. They explained that as the reason they had to have him in a special padded room. Second, they told us that he needed brain surgery or he would die. "Brain surgery? They're going to cut into his brain?" The doctor drew us a diagram to try to explain the procedure. How does a fifteen-year-old process this? I am not sure I ever did. I shut down even further. The roller-coaster ride was just too much, and I withdrew more than ever. Where had my invincible hero gone?

But what sticks with me the most about that time was sitting in the hospital waiting room while the doctors performed the twelve-hour brain surgery to repair the AVM (arteriovenous malformation), which had burst near the base of his brain. I had to be there. I just had to be in the same building. I waited for those twelve hours—thinking, wondering, and praying. The waiting was agony. There was nothing I could do to distract myself from the waves of "what ifs" that flooded my mind. There was only the pounding of my heart in my ears to remind me that this wasn't a dream. I couldn't read or watch TV. I just sat, waiting and staring at the gray wall in front of me. The wait still haunts me to this day. The anticipation every time the door swung open for an update. Exchanging glances with strangers in the room. Quickly hugging each other with our eyes since all of us waiting were in nightmares of our own. Holding our breath, waiting, hoping both for ourselves, for each other, and for our loved ones.

Finally, the moment came when the swinging door was for us. The doctor entered and declared, "He's in the recovery room now. It was a successful surgery."

I'd had this delusion that "success" meant he would return to us as we once knew him. "Thank God, the nightmare is almost over." However, it was merely the hopes and dreams of a teenager. The reality was that we no longer had the father we once knew. I had no idea it would be like this.

The first time I had a chance to see him, my heart broke into a million pieces. We had to dress in hospital gowns, masks, shoes, and gloves to protect him from infection. It was a full quarantine situation, and the very act of dressing into protective gear crumbled my delusional dream. The machines beeped and hummed. Dad looked like a science fiction experiment. White gauze wrapped around his head, tubes extruding from every direction. *Is he really alive? Is he in there?* I couldn't tell whether his hands were warm through the rubber gloves. Did he even know it was me since only my eyes were showing? I did everything in my power not to cry, but I could only hold the tears back for a few minutes before I had to leave.

After months in recovery and rehabilitation, it became a little easier visiting him. Our rerun reality show became more comfortable. When I saw what looked to me like a determined flicker of light in his eyes, I felt his fighting spirit breaking through. I felt hopeful. He had survived the brain surgery and a fierce fight with a staphylococcus infection. He had been through so much and seemed to take it all in stride. When they told us the brain surgery had been a success, I now realized that it meant he hadn't died on the operating table. What was clear was that life was going to be very different. Dad would be confined to a wheelchair for the rest of his life. If this wasn't bad enough, he was now also living with double vision, which meant he saw two of everything. The images he could see were forever to be stacked like a two-storey building. His newly limited speech capabilities meant he could no longer speak in lengthy sentences as most people normally do. And the body tremors meant he had trouble feeding himself because of his shaking arm. There was also short-term memory damage; he couldn't remember many daily details or whether we had come to visit him—though he did know who we were. His long-term memory was perfect. He had vivid recollection of details that were archived prior to the surgery. Added to the list was his throat paralysis; this made swallowing a challenge. He had to be very mindful when eating or drinking or he would risk choking or even worse, suffer the consequences of fluid entering his lungs. Lastly was his limited mobility; his balance was compromised so he could stand and take a few steps with help, but not on his own. He was now trapped in a body that didn't work the way he wanted it to. At that time, he was forty-three years old, only five years older than I am today. Where had the strong, feisty, fun-loving, creative, talented handyman I called my father gone? Would he ever even stand again? It took me seventeen years to answer those questions.

People have said about my dad, "Thank God he survived." I agree. Yes, I am grateful he survived, but I was also very angry. I grieve for what happened to him as I thought, *it isn't fair. Why do bad things happen to good people? Is this what I have to look forward to in life—grief and heartache?* Before my father's illness, I had thought I believed in God, so he took the brunt of my despair. "I hate you! You ruined my life, my family. Why would you do this to us?" But then again, I still prayed. It was the only thing I could do. The only thing that kept the very small pinhole of light present in the dark room of my existence.

There was another kind of grief I learned, different from the grief that is directly related to death itself. In my dad's case, this was the grief I felt over what Dad's reality used to be and no longer was. Back then, nobody talked about grieving for life as we had once known it. But I felt an immense amount of grief for the normal life that I envisioned I deserved. What if this had never happened? I wanted to somehow undo it all, and then I felt ashamed for thinking that. Nobody talked about what was happening, and thus I began to believe that grief was only reserved for death. He hadn't died, so I shouldn't be feeling what I was feeling. I feared some kind of judgement in that although he survived, I was still sad. Reason told me I should be grateful he was still with us in body. And yet I had thoughts that maybe he would have been better off if he had died on the operating table, since his future was going to be so full of what appeared to be insurmountable challenges. I felt guilty for having those feelings, so once again my emotional squirrel buried them deep. At fifteen years of age, I thought that I needed to be strong for my father—Dad as he now was. The problem was that my psychological squirrel was now in charge of defining what it meant to be strong—not me. "Be strong" is a catch phrase and what society seems to require of us. In retrospect, I didn't need to be strong. What I really needed was time to grieve over losing the dad I had once known and relied on. I needed help in connecting with the dad I now had. I didn't know how to express that need. Because no one talked about it, it appeared that no one else knew how to deal with it either. Most everyone expressed their relief that he survived, and then they went home and carried on with their lives. The doctors, nurses, and support staff had done their jobs—they stopped his bleeding brain—but in my life, the emotional bleeding had only just begun.

At the time, my parents were divorced and both in new relationships and life after his surgery felt a bit complicated. We were left as a blended family, trying to cope on our own. I lived with my mom full time, so learning how to relate to him, every second weekend, was another challenge for me. There wasn't much else I could do under those circumstances. As I look back, I am grateful that his fighting spirit and commitment to keep on going had given me seventeen years in which to get to know him again. I was given an opportunity to learn what it meant for Dad to "stand even" in the face of not being able to do so physically.

As a fragile teenage girl, none of this was the life lesson I was anticipating. I wanted to be like everyone else—"normal," free from a family that seemed to be crumbling at every turn. Other kids seemed to be leading blissful, carefree teenaged lives. Instead, my own view of the world changed, due at first to facing the possibility that my father might die, and then coming to terms with his subsequent survival as a person living with severe disabilities.

I sensed a growing heaviness on my shoulders with every experience. I certainly did not feel carefree or happy. I felt like I was living with a constant haze over my eyes, muting the colours and feelings of joy. I held a new belief about happiness; it came at a cost—so I had to always be on guard, watching for the one day when I might have to deflect any further bad things that might take it all away. The walls I built continued to grow taller as I pushed people away to protect myself from getting hurt again. "If you don't get close, you don't have pain." I played the Simon and Garfunkel song "I Am a Rock"[4] often, and it served as my mantra. I created that space as I continued to grieve alone. My emotional squirrel worked away tirelessly, burying my feelings.

I continued on. I had one-sided conversations with my classmates—in my mind. My perspective was shifting.

When the girls would complain about their problems with boys or issues with their hair or makeup, I would be thinking, *Yeah, well at least you can walk. At least you can speak in full sentences.* I was bitter and angry. *You guys have no idea what you have. You can feed yourselves, go to the bathroom, walk, and talk. My dad can't do any of those things.*

Ultimately, I hated being part of the pettiness of high school. It was a very lonely time for me. I never really talked it over with anyone. But nobody asked, either. Isn't that interesting? As I had hoped, I suppose I really had become invisible—but not entirely. I desperately wanted people to wake up and see how fortunate they were. I wanted to shake people and somehow give them a sip of my dad's reality. How could I make them see?

"Illness" is a poem I wrote in Grade 12. This was my way of offering a glimpse into my world. As I read it today, I see someone crying out for help, grief dripping from each word. It makes me a little sad now to think that I didn't have the courage to ask for the help I needed when I needed it. On the other hand, would I have taken that help if it were offered? I'm not sure, since I had already decided that I had to be my own version of strong, which meant stuffing my emotions away from sight. Do people who are carrying the illusion of being strong ask for help? Probably not. I hope this book encourages a great deal of reflection on that question. Right now, I just want to hug my seventeen-year-old self and tell her, "Hey, Life gets better. The haze will lift, I promise."

Illness

He sits silently,
Patient,
Longing to initiate a conversation, fails.
He stares into oblivion,
Scared.
Caged in an unfamiliar skeleton.
Same man, strange function.
A body dead like the eyes of a forgotten soul.
Lost.
To reach and feel the touch of someone's flesh
Is a task like a baby learning to speak.
This baby is a father—a man.
To express a single sentence—
Hours.
To make a tiny gesture—
Hours.
What is he thinking?
Unknown.
He sits silently.
If only the chains that glue him to his chair
Would break
Free.
Dare not look up,
Fear his eyes have vanished.
Dare not show weakness,
Fear people realize his disability.
Speak.
Embrace.
Walk.
PATIENT.
Silently sits.

Time passed, and gradually I became more comfortable with my circumstances. My thoughts began to change. I grew tired of carrying around the bitterness and anger. I wanted instead to create some kind of positive existence within this horrific reality. I began to wonder what it would be like if it were me who was in that predicament. How would I want those people I loved to feel? How would I want them to live and think about what had happened?

What would Dad want me to do? Would he want me to be this bitter? Or would he want me to be aware and grateful for what was real for me and what I had?

I knew I wanted to be the kind of person and student of life that I felt Dad would be proud of. I wanted to look back on my life and feel proud that I hadn't succumbed to the darkness. I suspect that I could have turned to drugs and alcohol to numb myself even further. Why did I say no to that option? Because I wanted to look my dad in the eye and have him feel uplifted by what I was creating, even with my heart being scattered in a million pieces.

I started the practice of noticing. The lens through which I saw life was one of being grateful for the simple things—like simply breathing, taking walks, and talking. This was to be my foundation. I decided to start living a richer life by trying out new things. Dad would want me to do this. He would want me to embrace every opportunity life offered. He would want me to embrace life and enjoy it. Jump on the Harley of life and be free. So I did. If nothing else, his reality awoke me to how precious life is. How each moment is a gift that we cannot take for granted. I learned at a very young age that if there was something I wanted to do, I had better do it now because one day I could wake up and discover, "I can't see."

I still feel the heaviness in my heart, even after Dad had passed away. I suppose it never truly goes away, at least not completely. Sometimes it shows up in waves and I am overcome. But then it eases and eventually dissipates. I live with it. More than that, I actually am grateful for it because I use it to honour my father. It has become Dad's reminder to me to live life to the fullest. He taps me on the shoulder quite often and whispers, "Write the book now, not tomorrow. Stop doing the dishes. Play with your girls. Get up on that stage and give that talk. Live your life and bring me with you on all your adventures. Fill up on new experiences."

When I see it all this way, it is a gift waiting to be explored and shared. I feel lighter. I breathe easier. The way I see it now is that I could spend my time trying to keep burying the pain of those years or I could carry forward the lessons I found and keep finding in the experiences I've had. I decided to let my mental squirrel go. There are no longer any more places to bury my emotions. Retire, dear friend.

Mentorship is about acknowledging there are lessons and using them to help us grow. This is a more powerful approach than living in the swirl of past stories, blame, and regret. My dad's illness was sad and tragic. It would be for any teenager. While I grieved his loss, I recalled all the times that we connected. I had an instinctive "knowing" about the importance of connection—a legacy Dad left me. Take the time to reflect on your greatest experiences. There is so much to learn and discover about who you are and what matters to you. What matters to me is all about that connection. That is what mentorship is about for me—pushing past the pain of the story and digging deeper to what matters.

Chapter Four

3 AM

Ever since Dad became sick, I'd felt the spark to write a book about my experiences of loving a parent who was living with severe disabilities. I didn't do it because, although I felt the story needed to be told, I was afraid of being too vulnerable. The little girl from Grade 5 surfaced and screamed, "No way! It's too risky!" I had built myself up as this strong young woman who could handle the prolonged illness and eventual death of her father. If I wrote a book, I would have to admit that I wasn't that strong, that the strength was just a character I was portraying. I would have to admit that I'd relied on my emotional squirrel to hide all the evidence of my pain so I could put on a smile. I would have to shine the light on the darkest parts of myself and admit that the definition of strength that ruled my life at the time was no longer serving me. My weakness was holding me back from living life fully. I would have to admit all the unhealthy strategies I had adopted to survive and that I was merely a shell numbly walking through life. I was unwilling to go to a place of strength because I wasn't willing to let go of my pain yet.

My definition of *strength* has changed considerably since my teenage days. Today, if you were to ask me for my view of strength, I would say it is a measure of how deeply I am willing to share myself. How deeply I am willing to feel and how I acknowledge my feelings. Whether I am willing to become vulnerable despite the tendency to want to rely on my trusted squirrel to collect and stuff away any pain. Writing this book has been incredibly healing. The act of sharing has helped repair my broken heart. The million little pieces are coming back together and I no longer feel broken. I feel inspired. Perhaps as a teenager my desire to write a book came from some innate knowledge that sharing would help me to heal. It took me over twenty years to act on this knowledge.

Through the years, even though I didn't write a formal book, I still wrote. I remember doodling in a notebook the idea of my first book that I would call *My Dad Can Still Give Me Hugs*. Instead of writing down what he couldn't do, I would write down all of the things he *could* do. Years later, after the difficult decision to move dad to a care home, my aunt hung a poster in Dad's room. It showed a dog balancing an apple on its nose. The caption was "Nobody can do everything, but everyone can do something."

Every time I went to visit, I would stare at that poster. It kept me aware of the important things that he *could* do. It brought me back to the lists I would make, doodling in my room. He could put his hand up as if to wave, if we waited long enough to see it. He could give us a hug, if we waited long enough to experience it with him. He could say I love you, if we waited long enough to hear it. His heart was beating, his mind was processing, he was here. Everyone who came in contact with him loved him instantly. His soul seemed to shine brighter after his surgery. There was a sense of ease that surrounded him. He taught me that there is power in being who you are, and that is sufficient. He showed me that we don't have to do anything to be "enough" in life. We don't need a fancy corporate title or millions of dollars in the bank. All we need is to be and feel sufficient inside. All we need to do is stand even on the inside.

I still talk to my dad. All the time. The lessons I chose for this book came out of one of those conversations while I was out of town attending a work conference. It had been a long day of leadership meetings, networking, and feeling overstimulated. I fell into bed, exhausted. Around 3:00 a.m., I awoke. I was five months pregnant with my second daughter and thought that was why I woke up. But it was something else. It felt like I was receiving messages—accompanied by a ringing in my head that was so loud I couldn't sleep. And I felt some kind of a palpable energy, as if I was vibrating. It was as though I had taken a double shot of espresso. The room was spinning a bit and I felt dizzy because of it. Three sentences were floating around in my head: "Take the time. It is nice to be seen. When it matters, say something."

"Dad?" Could it be?

Yes, it definitely was. After each statement a clear vision of an experience flashed in my mind. I saw it clearly, as if I had travelled back in time like the storybook entity of the ghost of Christmas past. Viewing it from above and taking note of the powerful moment in front of me.

I got out of bed and wrote for about an hour. I remember mumbling to my dad, "Whoa! Slow down! I can't keep up!" I felt his presence clearly for the first time since he passed, four years earlier. Since that night, I have had this overwhelming knowledge that I had to share his amazing wisdom. His journey, which once felt tragic, all of a sudden felt magical. This confirmed to me that our experiences really do matter. They have an impact on who we are—who we become—as human beings. Astonishingly, my father was mentoring me once again, and all I had to do was to be open to listening for the wisdom. I had to take the responsibility and accept that all I needed was myself. I had powerful lessons in me that could propel my life forward. Dad was shining the light on where I needed to dig. This was the day I retired that squirrel forever. It was time for me to start digging.

Although valuable, we don't necessarily have to have formal mentoring relationships, one-on-one meetings, or scheduled interactions in order to have a great mentorship learning experience. Much easier and often more effective is that we can each observe and ask ourselves, "What have I learned from the interactions I have already had in my life?" Then wait and see what bubbles up to the surface. I didn't have to force any answers. All I had to do was access one thing—silence.

Today, I intentionally carve out enough time to become quiet and listen deeply to what is going on inside me. Silence is such a gift. I live on a farm, surrounded by vast fields and sky, very different from the cookie-cutter subdivisions I had been accustomed to. Did I meet my husband, who happens to be a farmer, because I was destined to live where I do? Destined to be surrounded by silence in order to heal and find my voice again? I like to think so.

While now my favourite part about living here is the silence, it was the hardest thing to get used to. I had become desensitized to noise when I lived in the city, and I'd learned to function and be part of it without realizing its impact. So my new life, where there was silence, a lack of noise, somehow felt awkward—as if there were something wrong. I felt vulnerable without the noise. Where was the continuous bombardment of stimulus? Where were all the distractions? The vibrations that for years had attacked me from every angle were no longer present, and it felt odd for a long time.

After many months, I could finally hear myself, and I started to understand what *presence* really meant. I had to start listening. Being without the constant hum of the city for some time now, I began to enjoy that newly found sense of presence. I now appreciate and notice it. Often I will sit on my front step just to test what I can hear. One summer day all I heard were the buzzing bees. Imagine just hearing bees. It was amazing. In between the buzzing there were absolutely no sounds. Nothing, not even a bird chirping. I could only hear my heart beating and my breathing. What an extraordinary feeling—to be outside without the hum of traffic, sirens, and chatter. Silence is magical because it reminds me that I can only rely on myself for decisions, without the noisy opinions of others that tend to drag us off track. Silence sparks curiosity. I became lost in wondering whether the answers I was looking for would present themselves if I allowed myself a little bit of quiet time. I wondered whether that was why Dad's message showed up at 3:00 a.m. Was it because my world was so noisy I wouldn't otherwise have noticed it? Had it appeared before and I had ignored it? Yes, I admit I had ignored the tap on the shoulder in the past. This time I couldn't ignore it. He was no longer whispering; he was almost shouting.

After Dad passed away, I beat myself up for not asking him more questions. I kicked myself for spending our visits going for walks, watching movies, and playing cribbage instead of me asking him deeper questions about the meaning of life from his perspective. I had regrets about not investing the time in questions about his spirituality or his view of what had happened to him, particularly the path his life had taken before I was old enough to know him. Still, the night the messages came, I released all the guilty feelings. I realized that just by being in his presence and re-creating those memories, the answers were there, under the surface. He was showing me the answers and giving me glimpses by the phrases he chose to use in our conversations. I just had to reflect on our time together to get what I needed.

Dad and I didn't plan this. It happened organically. There were no checklists or mentorship models to follow. I was given exactly what I needed, when I needed it. My greatest mentorship experiences were the ones that flowed naturally, with the people who crossed my path unexpectedly. The learning was the most profound when I didn't force it but took the time to explore and unravel it as I applied it in my daily life. Maybe that's why I now feel that at certain times I came up short in parts of my career—I'd been trying to control and regulate a concept that perhaps needed more flexibility. Maybe with a little trust and intention, the right people show up when we need them most. I know that has been the case for me, whether it is in personal or professional growth.

The lessons in these three phrases shaped who I am today as a woman, wife, daughter, sister, parent, friend, and career woman. How come? Because they touched me at the core of who I am. They have proven to be profound and transformational. Dad had been mentoring me all of these years, but I hadn't realized it until that magical night when it all came together. I felt the power of the universe, the energy of everything around me, and it came together like a billion-piece puzzle. It all made sense, I felt an ease I hadn't felt before. I was connected to a powerful knowledge that everything was okay just as it was. I cannot explain it. I just knew it, and I felt the scattered pieces of my broken heart come back together as one, in a flash of healing light.

And now, on this journey of accessing my everyday mentors, I am being pulled to share, knowing that the impact will be greater than I can imagine. Share yourself and heal. Explore your powerful experiences. Share yourself, uncover who you are, and show the world the power of being your true self.

Chapter Five

Dig Deeper

Three short statements and a lifetime of discovery.

1. Take the Time

It is such a simple statement, yet seemingly so difficult to follow, especially in this modern world: take the time.

We have all heard it before in such clichéd phrases as "stop and smell the roses." We all know the importance of it, yet we continue to struggle and rarely stop and reflect—except maybe when we are forced to do so by some circumstance, most often health related. I have stopped relying on the drama of life events as a reason to slow down. I see it all around me—the life being sucked out of the people I care about as they desperately try to manage all of the external noise and expectations.

This is the number one topic I hear from my clients. Included are statements such as "I feel as if I don't have time for the things that matter to me"; "I'm exhausted and running on empty"; "I'm running around in circles"; "I'm uninspired"; "All I do is run and I have nothing left for my family when I get home."

The conversations always end up with an exploration of the same questions: What do you want to spend your time on? What matters most?

As I look back on my time with my dad, I am grateful that I had seventeen years of practice in "taking time." There was no other way for any of us to be when we were with him. Everything in his life took time—eating, speaking, moving—everything. In his world there was no rushing. I learned to wait, especially when we said goodbye. I would stand at the door and say, "Bye, Dad. I love you." He would slowly look up, left eye closed, head tilted to the left so he could focus past his double vision. He lifted his arm with an open hand as if to wave. I didn't leave until he finished his wave. It meant the world to me that he made the effort to do it, and I am sure it meant the world to him that I waited to receive it.

There was one thing he did do quickly, and it makes me smile to think of it. He could drink a cup of coffee at lightning speed. I have never seen anything like it. We would put a straw in his coffee cup and he would gulp it down without taking a breath. You could hear the coffee roll down his throat with every swallow. I recall watching him in awe, wondering how he could do that without burning his mouth. It was truly awesome. I guess he figured it would take too much time and effort to get the straw back if it slipped out of his mouth. Who wants to drink cold coffee anyway? Drinking a cup of coffee was a treat for him because he could do it without assistance. I like to think that cup of coffee symbolized empowerment and independence. But who knows? Maybe he just liked hot coffee rather than cold coffee. He was never one to complicate things.

Dad and his coffee-drinking performance reminds me of the Energizer Bunny that came out in 1989 and became popular in the early 1990s.[5] For whatever reason, Dad always loved that character from the Energizer battery commercials. After his surgery, this bunny character provided some ironic comic relief that we needed—as a family. His Christmas stocking had the Energizer Bunny on it, and I think he liked using this as his mascot. Dad's world grew slower and more difficult over the years because of his disability, but he just kept "going and going."

One of his biggest challenges was that he couldn't speak very well. His speech was like trying to talk while gargling mouthwash. His voice was rough and his words were very hard to understand. But he tried, and it took a lot of energy. To figure out what he was attempting to say, I would have to select from a series of strategies. Over and over, I would ask him to repeat a word. If that didn't work, we would play charades. First word, first letter is ... Then we would move on to the alphabet and say each letter, and he would put up a finger once we hit it. "Take a deep breath, Dad, and try again," I would often encourage. Once it took me an hour to figure out a couple of words in the sentence he was trying to say. When I finally figured it out, I realized he was trying to correct me. I had mentioned the wrong name of someone in a story I was reminiscing about. He still had his wits about him! I always encouraged him to finish his words, no matter how long it took for us to figure them out. I felt that what he had to say was important, and it mattered that we heard him.

One particular memory that has stayed with me was from my cousin's wedding. My father loved music. Before he became sick, he taught himself to play the guitar, banjo, and bass. He was also a very good dancer. He wasn't afraid to get out on the floor and shake it. I have fond memories as a kid, of us at the community hall, square dancing to Grandpa calling out the instructions.

We never wanted him to feel invisible or left out just because he was in a wheelchair. Whenever we were doing things together as an extended family, we did our best to include Dad. At the wedding, after the dance had started, I asked him if he wanted to go onto the dance floor. "Yes," he nodded. With the help of my two aunts, I stood him up in the middle of the dance floor. I took one side, my aunts took the other sides, and we held him in a semicircle of support. I am sure he would have made a joke about how much these three women wanted to dance with him. He tried moving his feet a little as we held him. The four of us swayed back and forth as one.

After the song ended and we gently guided him back into his chair, he kept trying to say something. None of us could understand him; all I could hear was the gargling sound. He kept repeating it. Since the room was very loud, we took him into the foyer of the hotel. We tried to make out his words. We went through our list of strategies and had him spell some words and repeat them. It must have been at least twenty to thirty minutes but finally we got it. He gargled out the words "Godspeed … his … love … to … me. " He must have said that sentence a hundred times before we understood it.

I remember beginning to cry because I assumed he was trying to say something like "I like this song" or "I'm tired." I was speechless, as though I had landed on my back and the wind had been sucked from my lungs. All I could do was tell him that I loved him and give him a big hug. The sentence "Godspeed his love to me," spun around in my head for the rest of the evening and has never left me.

I will never know what was going on in his mind that had inspired this statement. Was he asking for God's love in that moment? He was not part of any organized religion and did not seem to be religious at all. We never had a chance to talk about his spiritual beliefs. All I could figure was that he was moved by something that happened in that moment on the dance floor. This experience plays in my memory as a reminder of what we are missing by not taking the time with people. It doesn't matter to me what he meant by the statement because obviously in that moment it meant something important to him. It does matter a great deal to me that I stuck with him and had a chance to hear him say what he said.

The lessons from this experience helped create the foundation for my career as a coach and leader and most importantly, for my personal life. My new mantra became "take the time, and don't give up on people." Everyone deserves to be heard, no matter how hard it may be to understand them, whether it is their language, culture, belief systems, or a disability. When you take the time to listen, profound and magical things happen. You experience people deeply and your relationships flourish. All people want is to be heard and loved. This takes time and your investment in them.

My dad surprised me so deeply that I had an emotional, visceral response. It was so unexpected that it felt like a shock to my system. I learned that you never know for sure what is going on in someone's mind. Don't assume you know what is important to someone else. The only way you will ever know is to be curious and ask questions. Each person deserves the respect of having his or her own way of feeling and thinking. We don't have the right to impose our perspective on others. Wipe away your own assessments and let others take the stage. This is why I think I make a good coach and leader. I don't make up my mind about anything until I feel I have fully heard the other person's point of view. Even then, I stop my swirl of opinion because there is always more to discover. It is more about offering people a space in which to be heard more clearly rather than having an opinion about what they have already said. It will always be worth the wait and the time you invest.

It wasn't just about the words Dad spoke that evening. It was the entire experience of physically moving off the dance floor and focusing our attention. I often think back to the dance floor as a metaphor for our lives. The dance floor can be a lot of fun. It is loud, busy, and exciting. But if we are not careful, it can also be tiring, overstimulating, and overwhelming. We can get lost on it. Too often we become stuck in the crowd of dancers and forget that we need to pull ourselves off the floor from time to time to rejuvenate. To access that beautiful, rejuvenating silence. To access ourselves again.

What is going to take you off the dance floor? What needs your attention and reflection? I think those who rest between songs and take the time to invest in what they have learned have the richest of lives. I love the dance of life, and I also love the silence in the time off the floor.

2. It Is Nice to Be Seen

Dad didn't say too much after his surgery. The years I had with him were mostly taken up with us sitting together in silence, just enjoying being in the same room. He was a whiz at trivia and mental games and he never missed *Wheel of Fortune* on TV. I have many fond memories of watching it with him. We would also play cribbage. Grandpa built him a cardholder out of wood so he could play cards on his own. I would place the cards in the holder and he would point to the cards he wanted to play. He beat me ninety percent of the time.

One of the memories I cherish was watching classic movies together with Dad like *Uncle Buck*[6] or *Trains, Planes and Automobiles*,[7] and hearing him laugh. It wasn't a little giggle and it didn't happen often, but when he laughed it was amazing because it was so contagious. When he started, we would all have to laugh too. It was a laugh from the very core of his being. It was loud, guttural, and carefree. It came with ease and was beautiful, since talking was so challenging. I miss that laugh.

But what I remember most about our visits was his opening line. I would come in and always say, "Hi, Dad. It's so nice to see you."

His response, in a very slow deliberate voice, was, "It … is … nice … to … be … seen!"

This never changed. He said it every single time. It is funny when I think of it now. Most people would probably respond by saying, "It's nice to see you too." He never said that. I often think he was trying to teach me something by saying this, and it worked. That simple statement transformed how I interact with others. After all, isn't that what everyone wants in life—to be seen and to be acknowledged? Don't we want people to take the time to care about what we think and what is important to us? This is how I approach the people I encounter, whether a cashier at a store, the people I work with, or my family and friends. My intention with every interaction is to look them in the eye, be present, and make an effort to truly see and hear them.

As the years went by, I began to notice that beneath Dad's disability he was the same man and father. I just had to take the time to see past the physical body and look further into his being. With others, I now look for the little, simple things that make us who we are, rather than the masks and labels in which we cocoon ourselves. How easily we judge other people or situations based only on what we see visually.

I took my father out for lunch one day, which, I admit, was not easy. It was both mentally and physically demanding to go out into the world with Dad by myself. The most time consuming was getting him into the car safely, but I know he appreciated the effort because he said thank you often when we finally had ourselves settled in the car. I remember swallowing back tears many times after he would say it. One warm summer day, we were sitting on a restaurant patio having fish and chips. I had to help feed him so it took time for him to eat the meal. One deliberate bite and chew at a time. An elderly woman approached us. "It is so nice of you to do what you are doing," she said, walking away before I had a chance to respond.

It took me by surprise because I was simply having lunch with my dad and never considered what others were observing. I suppose people saw only a young woman sitting with and feeding a person in a wheelchair. I appreciate that she took a moment to share what she was feeling, and I would have also appreciated a moment to let her in on my experience. It reminded me once again that so much more lies behind most visual experiences. I would have loved it if the woman had asked me about our story. I think this is what Dad was trying to teach me. "Seeing" is about digging deeper and not making your decisions based solely on what is presented on the surface. Dad couldn't talk well, but he was an intelligent, loving, witty man once you spent some time around him and took notice. I think he wanted to be seen as someone more than just a man living with a disability. He wanted me to look past what I saw on the outside and focus on all the brilliance underneath.

In order to "see" people or allow ourselves to be seen, we have to be vulnerable, honest, and raw. We have to share our heart, our stories, and be open to feeling all of what life has put in our path. We cannot hide behind our armour or the brick walls we create around us. It takes courage and strength to truly be seen on the inside, and I am grateful for my dad's lesson—or I might not have written this book.

This lesson of "it is nice to be seen" became most evident once I started coaching. I feel very privileged that I get to "see" people in my work every day. I am reminded of a client who was guarded with many walls and would do everything in her power not to cry in our conversations. One day, I asked her, "What if you just let yourself cry?" and she burst out into what she called "the ugly cry." It was the most amazing, beautiful expression of what was happening in her heart at that moment. A moment where words were not necessary and I saw and felt her strength and power. I am inspired by feeling whatever is happening in the moment and offering people a space to be seen as they are, wherever they are at in their lives. Dad taught me how to create that for others and for myself. He taught me how nice it is to be seen and how nice it is to see others.

3. When It Matters, Say Something

Dad was always full of surprises. It was August 12, 2007, and I was in my hometown, starting my drive to my mother's house after the wedding of some dear friends. I lived out of province with my fiancée, so I didn't see Dad as much as I wanted, although I was committed to seeing him every month. I was making plans to see him the next day when the phone rang. Dad had been rushed to the hospital. I had always wanted to believe in divine intervention and this incident made me a believer. Why today? Why, just when I happened to be home? I was only thirty minutes away from the hospital. Dad had a severe case of pneumonia most likely due to his swallowing challenges. Once I arrived, the doctors were doing nothing. The nurse showed me a "Do

Not Resuscitate" order in his file, which was the first time I had heard about the existence of this document.

Where the hell did that come from? Why was I not informed? What is happening? The questions frantically filled my head.

"Why are you not intervening?" I asked.

"We can't," she said with an appearance of deep concern.

I started to panic because, dammit, I knew my father wanted to live. "I have power of attorney. Will you honour his wishes if I ask him?"

"Yes, if we feel he understands."

Dad was semiconscious. I asked him quietly, "Dad if you can hear me, nod your head." He nodded slightly. "Dad, do you want the doctors to do anything and everything possible to save your life?" He nodded up and down. A clear yes.

I looked at the doctor and they went to work. He was intubated once again.

I don't think my dad would have survived if I hadn't been there in that moment to ask the question. For the next month, he was hooked up to every life support machine imaginable. I had almost lost him again and was devastated.

I flashed back to my fourteen-year-old self once again. I relived the moment of crawling up the basement stairs. The fear came rushing in. *Is this it? This is it.*

Once again I found myself taking the same drive I had with my grandparents to go visit him. I held his hand in silence, rubbed lotion on his feet, and was there for him. For someone who had been through so much I was still in awe of his fighting spirit. The Energizer Bunny still going, fighting to squeeze more power from the battery. There were times as I sat watching his chest rise and fall with the machine that I felt guilty. *Should I have just let him go? Was it fair that he had to be in this place again? But he had decided for himself*, I thought. He wanted to be here for a reason. I saw it in his eyes. Maybe he actually remembered that I was getting married. Maybe he wanted to be at my wedding, which was only eight months away. Just maybe he remembered more than I thought was possible. He made it, and it was to be the scene for the last of the three-part message.

I suspect every daughter dreams of walking down the aisle on her father's arm. I did. It is such a special moment and I didn't think my dad was going to be there—his episode with pneumonia had taken a great toll on him physically. He was there and he "wheeled" me down the aisle, his hand in my hand. He sat there, silently contented, as my brother managed his wheelchair.

The justice of the peace acknowledged him. "Who gives this woman to be married to this man?"

There was a short pause. The hall fell silent as everyone held their breath. Dad took a deep breath and bellowed, *"I do!"* in a clear, loud voice. There was no gargle, no hint or doubt or hesitation. I don't think there was a dry eye in the place. Surprised and holding back tears, I felt a wide smile cross my face. I will never forget that moment when my father wanted to make damned sure he was heard.

I looked at my husband-to-be and thought, *Well, I guess he approves.*

This moment was especially powerful. It taught me that when it matters, be sure you are heard. When it matters, say something. Stand up, stand even, and speak up for what you believe in. I am naturally a quiet, introverted person, and it has taken me a long time to feel worthy enough to speak my mind. I often think back to this experience in my moments of doubt and ask myself, "How important is this to me?" If it is important, I take a deep breath like my dad did, and I say something. The breath is not about mustering up the courage to speak. It is about giving myself that quick moment to say, "I am enough, and my voice is important." It is important for me to be heard, not to change an outcome or be the centre of attention. It is about standing up for what is important to me. It is about respect and inclusion. Everyone should have an opportunity, a voice. It is about honouring the fact that we all have experiences and wisdom to share, and it is important that we are provided a space in which to speak our truth.

I often wonder if, in the moment when my dad shouted out, "I do," it caused others to become emotional because they felt the power of what he had accomplished. I think he struck a nerve with others because they saw the possibility of overcoming obstacles when it matters to them. They witnessed a man become capable, someone they may have assumed was not able. I wonder if the tears were triggered because we realized that we often sit in silence and don't say anything. I wonder if the tears were for all the lost moments of not honouring what matters to us.

For goodness sake, say something. Imagine what would be possible if you said what matters to you. Dad fought back from certain death once again and bellowed out, "I do." The energy of his words was so magical it resonated throughout the entire hall. It was so much more than the words, "I do." It was determination, possibility, and most of all, it was love.

My wedding day—2008.

Chapter Six

Legacy

The last time I saw Dad looking reasonably healthy, given his circumstances, was at my wedding. He continued to struggle after his battle with pneumonia. Due to his progressively worsening paralysis, he was put on a feeding tube. This meant that he had to forego the joy of tasting his food and especially his beloved cup of coffee. He became bedridden because the tube feeding was difficult to regulate. He seemed to have one challenge after another. His weight skyrocketed, and it became too difficult for me to take him outside for our usual spin around the block. He was too big for his wheelchair; this was difficult to witness.

As I continued to visit, I could see the light in his eyes becoming dimmer. His energy was changing, and although he tried to engage, it wasn't the same. I felt tired for him, and every time I went to visit, the heaviness of his situation became more unbearable to me. I cried in my car many times, praying for strength. One day, at the end of a visit, I whispered in his ear that if he wanted to go, it would be okay and we would all understand. I knew his body was getting very tired of fighting. I also knew he would keep going as long as he could—after all, he idolized the Energizer Bunny.

The last time I saw Dad was in late October 2009, as my husband and I were preparing to go on our long-awaited three-week honeymoon to Australia. I remember telling him I couldn't wait to get back so I could tell him about it and show him the pictures we would take. I asked him if he would like that. He nodded yes. I wanted to have rich experiences so I could share our joy with him. When our plane landed back in Canada, the flight attendant announced that they had a message for me. I was to call home immediately. They don't page passengers on a flight unless they have been given an important reason for doing so. I knew it was about Dad. I couldn't stop crying as I made my way through customs. I had to wait to make that call since cell service was not available until we made our way out. Yes, the message was about Dad. He passed on November 21, 2009.

When I arrived home, my brother asked me if I'd received his email. "No! What email?" As it turned out, he had been emailing me at the same time that I was emailing him. I had logged on to a boarding-lounge computer and was informing my family that we were on our way home. At the time, I thought it was weird that as soon as I clicked "Send," the computer I was using suddenly logged me off and went black. I didn't have time to find another computer to log back in. My brother told me he emailed me literally seconds after my message popped up on his screen. Dad was dying and he was heading to the airport right away to be with him.

I often wonder if Dad had a part to play in turning that computer off. Did he somehow know? Did he plan to spare me a fifteen-hour flight that would include me beating myself up because I wasn't there with him? And perhaps he didn't want me to berate myself for having gone on the trip in the first place? As I look back on my experience in the airport that day, the computer was only one sign of what was to come. I was an emotional wreck that day. At first I thought it was just because I was tired from the long trip, but I think I must have felt him passing on. We were checking in, and the agent informed us there were no seats together. I lost it to the point of having to leave the area. I went into the bathroom and sobbed uncontrollably for what felt like an eternity. I couldn't control my emotions. My body was shaking and I felt out of control. I even asked myself—*really Kim, over a couple of seats?* I didn't understand what was happening until I heard the announcement and it all became clear. I had somehow known.

Yes, I was devastated by his death, but there was also a wave of relief that he was finally free from the chains of his body. His soul was finally free to dance, play his guitar, and ride his Harley on the whispers of the wind. I am sad not to have him with me in body, but I always knew that I could take him wherever I went in my life. He is with me and he continues to mentor me with his powerful legacy of "Take the time. It is nice to be seen. When it matters, say something."

Part Three

My Awakening

Chapter Seven

The Bee Sting

Mentorship is a complicated phenomenon. We usually think of mentors as people whom we greatly admire—those people who reflect back to us a life we strive to emulate and create. While I choose to surround myself with the people who inspire me, I also know that all lessons are valuable, especially ones that seem painful at first glance. My experience with my dad was painful in many ways, but he wasn't a painful person. Painful people are here to test us. They challenge us and test whether we are willing to stand up for what matters. Are we willing to put ourselves first? For me, a painful experience is like getting stung by a bee. Our job in life is noticing the difference between a bee sting from a painful experience and a sting from a painful person. They feel very different and are powerful mentorship opportunities just the same.

Many of us wear our pain like a suit of armour. Some of us become so engulfed by it that it masks who we truly are. We start to make all our choices through the experience of pain, creating more and more as we move through life. When the pain becomes a huge burden, we end up treating people poorly or tolerate people treating us poorly. I get that. I was in a place like that. While it is a challenge pulling out of the tornado of pain and anger, I can attest that it is possible.

Part of the process in my learning was to be fundamentally okay with what happened to my dad. Without knowing it, while he was mentoring me in learning how to reconnect with him, he also taught me how to be with my pain. His health struggles nudged me into learning more about myself and what makes me tick. The last twenty-four years has been an intense course on how to manage emotional pain. How to cope with tragedy, how to survive, how to heal, and how to be light in the midst of all the dark.

He opened this door for me when I wasn't sure I would have asked him to, given a choice. I had to decide whether I wanted to be the hamster on the wheel of pain. I had to decide whether I wanted to be defined by these events in my life. I am grateful I chose to walk through the door he left open for me. While living under this burden of pain and heartache is hard, it doesn't have to be that way forever. We can walk with it rather than be crippled by it. Since Dad didn't seem to cloak himself in what had happened, I finally decided I didn't want to either. I didn't want to be a painful person, dragging people into my misery, so I had to make my choice. Life started opening up for me once I decided to accept that the pain happened, it was painful, and now it was time to move on, learn from it, and create an extraordinary life.

I am grateful that I had my dad to show me that, "You don't have to wallow in your grief, Kim." Grief can evolve and grow into inspiration. I learned to move with the pain like a dance and be at peace with it. Our experiences do not have to weigh us down forever. Life's "bee stings" are amazing opportunities to react in ways that have us grow and learn. I would not be able to appreciate the light if I hadn't allowed myself to walk in the dark sometimes. I don't fight the dark days any longer—I allow them. I use them as a tool, wearing them fully and with awareness. I look at them deeply and pick out the best that I can find in them for myself for when the lightness returns. This is where my greatest learning has been.

One of the ways I learned how to use the bee sting analogy and discover the lesson is to remove myself from the equation. I picture myself in a university lecture hall surrounded by other eager students. I then imagine that a well-respected professor is presenting his years of study on the subject related to what I am struggling with.

I ask myself, "What is the professor trying to teach me? What am I supposed to be learning from this? What is the bigger picture here?"

By creating a neutral scenario, I can see my experience in a new way. It provides me with an opportunity to see the experience as a lesson from which to learn, rather than an experience in which I might become emotionally entangled. It is one way to unplug the ego, unplug the tendency to play the victim or become caught up in the "poor me" syndrome. It is easy to get lost in that particular game, and it is especially easy to point fingers at people who are also stuck. These days, I like to spend more of my time in the university lecture rather than in the drama of stories and assumptions.

I remember an instance when I used this idea with one of my clients. He was in a swirl about his father. I could hear the hurt, frustration, and betrayal in the story he shared. It was a very painful sting. I asked him to imagine he was sitting in a classroom and that his father was up at the front, teaching a class about the situation, including the reasons why he acted the way he did.

What would the theme of the class be? What was at the root of the situation from the perspective of his values?

My client's eyes widened. I could definitely see a shift in his perceptions. He had reached an internal understanding he never knew existed for him. He said, "Although I don't agree with how he went about it, I can see now that he was coming from a place of love." The hurt was still there, but an expanded understanding of another's point of view was now included. This insight provided him with an opportunity to reconnect and have further conversations from a different viewpoint. He was able to consider that he wasn't the only one who experienced a painful sting. He was willing to see that there was more to explore and learn from his experience.

My depth of awareness was born in the processing of "bee sting" lessons. I know exactly what it feels like to be stung, and I now know how to move through it. I have been there many times and will be there many more times, I'm sure. It is part of being human, part of living life, and I accept all of it. What I am most grateful for is that I now know how to recognize a "painful" person and can choose whether I am willing to be stung. I see the bee coming these days! I cannot always anticipate the sting of painful experiences, but I am equipped with tools to be able to move through them in a healthy way.

Dad opened up the opportunity for me to nurture my awareness. To live a life, awake and present so I have the power to create something amazing out of all my experiences, whether they are labelled as good, tragic, transformational, or uneventful. I learned that it isn't always about me and what I am feeling. There are many moving parts to every circumstance, and I had to realize that my perspective was merely mine and everyone else has a perspective as well. It was only fair for me to honour perspectives rather than just conclude whether I deemed something right or wrong. We can evolve into so much more if we just let go of our own stories and accept that our perspective is only one piece in a complex puzzle of the human experience.

Chapter Eight

Let Go

If the people in our world don't fill us up, then we have to let go of their impact on our lives. Letting go is an intention, a choice we are making. It is a shift in how we view our experiences and how we deal with the grip they have on us. I held on to a lot of anger and disappointment with people during my dad's journey with his health. I was angry with many who said they cared but had a funny way of showing it, at least in my view.

Letting certain toxic people and experiences go is such a rewarding concept, but it takes courage, awareness, and intention. It is easier to live in the swirl of stories and the drama about what others have "done" to us. What is true is that holding on to drama robs us of the opportunity of experiencing life to the fullest. Letting go is really about putting yourself first and focusing on what you need in order to move your own life forward. I think this is especially true for women because many of us believe it is selfish to put ourselves first. For some reason, we seem to have held on to this collective belief, but as I look around at the community of women in my life, I am pleased to witness we are loosening the grip. I am grateful to be part of a generation in which we are recognizing the value of caring for ourselves first so we can care for others more effectively.

I noticed the bubble of anger and resentment surface during my journey with Dad, and yet I also noticed that he didn't seem to hold those same feelings in the same way. In my family, we always teased one another about getting a little hot under the collar at times. Even Dad. And yet after his surgery, I never witnessed any of those eruptions. He seemed to be in a steady state of "going with the flow." It occurred to me that his brain injury and limited short-term memory might have been an unexpected gift. Maybe he couldn't hold on to emotions and experiences as I did. Maybe his brain wouldn't let it happen, so, in his way, he mastered the art of letting go and living in the present. His ability to stay present without the burden of memory allowed for his true self to shine through. What a gift!

As for me, I realized over time that it was very unhealthy to hold on to the anger I was harbouring because it prevented me from living the fullest expression of my life. It was sucking all my energy and time. For what? I also came to realize that my anger was mainly due to my immediate perception of the situation. I never asked any of the people I was upset with why they acted and responded as they did. I was having a one-sided conversation based only on my specific experiences and judgements, and those were based on my assessment that certain people weren't around as much as I thought they should be. Have you ever caught yourself having a conversation with someone who wasn't actually there? This is what I mean by a one-sided conversation. Yet somehow we believe we have interacted and our emotions about the situation get stronger without having their side of the story. This is a dangerous and toxic place in which to live. It is a very narrow and selfish reality. I didn't want to be a person who wasn't willing to admit

I had a part to play in all my experiences. I contributed as much as anyone did to the drama in my life, and once I owned up to my part, I was able to let go and forgive.

I recall hearing one of my dad's friends say that it was too difficult for them to visit him. Since Dad had been so full of life before, they couldn't bear to see him as he now was. This sparked a rage in me that I held on to for years. After I let it go, I came to understand that the comment had nothing to do with my dad. I suspect that it was merely their own fear of reality, fear of their own mortality, fear of the unknown. I guess I will never really know what story they told themselves. I can only theorize that Dad's condition reminded people that life is unpredictable and uncomfortable. It was their choice to live with the perspective they held that kept them away, and it was okay even if I didn't agree. I grew tired of having one-sided conversations in my mind with them about how wrong they were and how disrespectful I felt they were being. I came to a place of acceptance that everyone has a right to choose. I was left with just feeling sad that they missed knowing my dad in a new and lovely way. It was what it was. I made my choice and they made theirs.

What I witnessed from my father's friendships highlighted a very valuable lesson. Genuine, deep, life-long friendships are less plentiful than we imagine them to be. When times get tough we find out who is truly with us for the long haul. When tragedy strikes, we find out even more clearly who will stand with us. I watched as people slowly drifted away. I suspect they thought of us often and wondered how we were doing, but those who acted on those thoughts became fewer and fewer. But I also saw people step up, those who I never expected would do so. Lasting friendship is rare and precious—and I learned people flow in and out of our lives continuously. I learned to accept this flow in my own life and not beat up on myself for the times I have drifted away. I have since learned the art of letting go of people and being okay when they decide it's time to move on. I wish them well, grateful we had a connection even if only for a short time. I am proud of letting go of my belief that in order to be "somebody" I need a long list of friends. I feel content in the flow of friendship knowing some connections will last the test of time and some won't – it's okay either way.

When I visited Dad in the care home, I would notice, sadly, that many residents rarely had visitors. My hunch is that people stay away because visiting stirs up similar uncomfortable feelings and fears. I admit I hated going to the home because of how emotional it was for me. But once I got out of my own way and understood that I wasn't just visiting my loved one—I was part of a complex community. I was in the presence of so many souls whose lives had been turned upside down, whether by age or by some disease—and they all deserved to be seen. I would take a deep breath and walk in, knowing this visit wasn't about how I felt. It was about Dad and supporting his community, so my commitment to those visits remained strong. I would always smile as warmly as I could and fully acknowledge the others in the building even if only for a quick moment.

At the end of my visit I would go out to my car and cry all the way home. A tear for each interaction and for each person whose struggle was real. Crying seemed to be the release I needed so that I could go back one more time.

If one day I stumble upon a magic genie in a bottle, I have just one wish. I wish my dad were here to teach a class in letting go. What he had to face would probably be enough to illustrate the whole concept. Can you imagine him sitting in his wheelchair at the front of the class, in silence, while you read the following list from the chalkboard? He would sit there, quietly nodding his head in full understanding, and maybe he would eventually muster up the words, "It is nice to be seen, thank you."

- Let go of walking
- Let go of talking
- Let go of feeding yourself
- Let go of food
- Let go of steady hands
- Let go of clear vision
- Let go of memory
- Let go of independence
- Let go of relationships as they once were
- Let go of driving and riding
- Let go of working
- Let go of hobbies
- Let go of conversation as it once was
- Let go of what society defines as a contributing human being
- Let go of the dreams you had for your life
- Let go of the fact that someone else had to write this list on the chalkboard
- Just be, accept, and breathe

When you reflect on this list, what is left in one's life? If you were in this position, how would you want people to feel in your presence? That was what was left for my dad. The care aides and nurses would always tell me how much they enjoyed being around my dad even though he didn't say much. They felt him, and his soul. He still connected deeply with people and didn't have to do anything but simply be. He was contributing to this world in an extraordinary way because of how people felt in his presence. He was still connecting with us powerfully.

Most of us seek our worth in our jobs, the things we are able to do, how many credentials or things we accumulate. I know I lived a big portion of my life striving for success in my job so I could feel important. Waiting for that next opportunity to move up the corporate ladder, be paid more to have more, and finally feel fulfilled. It never happened, and eventually I realized my mentor had the answer. Dad could define himself by who he was only at his core. That is why, despite all his challenges, people loved him and enjoyed his company. He was a special person and didn't have to *do* anything to be special—simply *be*. We become caught up in thinking we have to do all sorts of things in life to be considered worthy. Dad taught me that just being here on earth, being who I am, and investing in what is important to me is enough.

I ask myself—do I feel worthy today? I try to invest in shedding all the stuff society piles on top of me—all the *shoulds* and *why don't you*s flying around. I know feeling enough is a work in progress, and I am constantly making advances. Dad reminds me to always be present and be willing to shed any labels that I may be carrying around as worthiness. Writing this book is one more step in my process of letting go—stripping myself down to just *being* and looking at what matters to me and my life.

Letting go, although simple in concept, is probably one of the hardest things we may have to learn to do as we go through life. People often say, "You've got to just let it go." *Just?* We let it roll off our tongue as if it is easy or that it should *just* happen. If dwelling on stuff was an Olympic sport, I am sure I would be a returning gold medalist. I am proud to say that I am getting further away from that "dwelling" podium. Letting go takes a great deal of daily effort, awareness, and intention. Learning to let go is an individual process; it takes time to figure out a practice that works best for each of us. It took me around thirty years, but I finally discovered my own process. I feel amazingly freed up because I am no longer a slave to my belittling thoughts, the expectations of others, and painful experiences.

How did all of this come to me? Much of it became clear as I watched both my mother and father struggle with their health. I got to witness the challenges and the power of letting go. I knew that letting go was powerful, but I struggled with *how* to do it.

What did it mean to let go? How could I do it so it would last? I needed someone to show me how to access a process. I believe from my own experience that when you ask for guidance, the right person or an unexpected invitation will show up. When you are ready, the mentor you need will be there to take your hand and walk with you. And as always, it did.

By a *chance* series of events, I had the privilege of experiencing a letting-go process in a workshop called "Authentic to the Core."[8] It was here that I began uncovering the layers of who I am. The fog that overshadowed my life began lifting. This workshop retreat taught me how to make sense of my experiences, especially those associated with my dad. I saw how important and powerful letting go could be. It was here that the pieces of my life's puzzle started coming together. It opened up my soul. I rediscovered that little girl, who she was before her voice was silenced. As I let go of that painful experience, I found my voice again and with that, my purpose. Letting go for me is about trial and error. I tried many different kinds of practices and rituals before I found something that felt right for me. I have always felt connected to the four elements (fire, water, earth, and wind) because being in nature is important to me. The letting-go processes I learned focused on that connection. The path was in front of me once again, and all I had to do was decide to step onto it. For me, letting go has to be an experience. I have to see it, feel it, and be part of it. My mind and body have to believe I am serious about moving forward. And this workshop paved the way for me to finally let go of all the experiences that had defined my existence so I could finally discover who I really was underneath. It was truly transformational. I woke up.

One of the exercises in the retreat was very meaningful to me. The facilitator, Lori Anne Demers, held up a glass. What she said about it has forever changed my perspective and my relationship with my experiences. It was so powerful it is worth sharing again. She asked us to pick up a glass and hold it tightly. She then asked us to try to pick up something else with the same hand. Obviously, my grip was so tight that I couldn't pick up anything.

She explained, "When we hold our experiences so tightly, we do not have room to experience anything else." She then asked us, concerning the glass, "Who is controlling whom? Can you see who or what is in control? In this scenario there is no place for anything else to show up. No choices, that's for sure. Your only choice is to continue to hold the glass. There is no space for creativity or growth. You can hold the glass tightly, loosely, or you can put it down. If you put it down, you now have a chance to make some choices. You can alter your experience with the glass by putting it down and allowing new opportunities to fill the space where the glass had been."

It struck me that I was denying myself new experiences because I was holding tightly on to the fourteen-year-old girl who went through a painful experience. What's true is that our experiences and our attachments to things will always be there. We get to decide how tightly we want to hold on to them. I can loosen my grip on them, when and if I choose to do so. It allows me to take my power back so I am not constantly sucked into the swirl of my story of the past. I don't have to overcome anything; I just have to decide and then put the story down for a while. My experiences are part of me, but they aren't who I am, so they don't have to rule my present. They can sit beside me in the university lecture hall, and I can move seats and change my perspective if I choose. The glass will always be there, and I get to decide what kind of relationship I want with it. This concept helped me to see my journey with my dad in a new light. I don't have to be crippled by it; I can be inspired by it. I can set the glass down; I can pick it up if I want to. I picked up my dad's glass often as I wrote this book, yet I felt differently this time. It was comforting, not painful.

When I am faced with a tough life experience, I always think of the journey I walked with my father. I compare it to a spiritual pilgrimage others embark on, but I did so over twenty-four years without having to get on a plane, wear a backpack, or walk a thousand miles. I know I can handle anything life may throw at me because of my expanded perspective.

One of the toughest and most recent experiences I endured occurred when my husband and I decided we wanted to have a second child. We became pregnant right away, but eight weeks later, I miscarried. I was upset with the loss, but I trusted that my body knew what was best for the baby and me. I was able to move on and let go quite quickly. A few months later, as the New Year began, we called it "our new year." We were given a fresh start. I was pregnant again, but after a few weeks, things went wrong again. I began having pain and ended up having an ectopic pregnancy. It hit me very hard, so much so that I started to have doubts about whether we would ever be able to have another child. I felt betrayed by life and found myself heading down a similar rabbit hole of despair. I felt similar feelings that hadn't presented themselves for years. I prayed to my dad a lot during this time. I prayed for his guidance and strength. I prayed for him to take care of the children we had lost. I prayed for comfort and resilience. I prayed for acceptance for where I was at. I prayed. I thought continually about my dad's own journey of letting go, and I knew I needed to do something similar in order to heal and move forward once more. I knew I had to get to a place where I accepted life as it was rather than feeling stuck in the desire for what I thought was best for me. I no longer wanted to feel frustrated for not having any control. I didn't want to be crippled with envy of others. I just wanted to feel enough with what was in front of me. I needed to let go.

One warm day in June, I was at the lake with my two-and-a-half-year-old daughter. We were sitting on our dock, just the two of us, throwing shale rocks into the water. My daughter loved how they splashed and rippled. She would scream with joy as each one hit the water. "Look at that splash!" she squealed with delight. In that moment, I decided to do a letting-go ritual. I was ready. Shale is very soft and the pieces we were throwing had large enough surfaces that I could write on them using the edge of a stone. I wrote every thought and word that came into my mind about having another child. I included my sadness about the two pregnancies that ended within six months of each other.

I wrote:

- Let go of the idea of a second child
- Let go of expectations
- Let go of my idea of the perfect family

- Let go of my anger, pain, resentment, grief
- Let go of any blocks to my healing
- Let go of mistrust
- Let go of control
- Peace
- Harmony
- Trust
- New possibilities

And so on…

I wrote my phrases on over thirty rocks. Laughing and enjoying the excitement and wonder in my daughter's eyes, we threw them together as far as we could. The ritual made me feel happy and relieved. I completely let go of the painful experiences and the attached grief. I was left feeling at peace with whatever direction life took me. I was fully present with the life I had now and was no longer caught up in a life I thought I should have. I trusted life again and the power of living in the flow rather than fighting to create what I thought was best. I felt whole. It was a beautiful, healing moment that I shared with my daughter. Even though she didn't know what I was doing or all the reasons, she supported me through it by being herself. It was brilliant.

A few weeks later, much to my surprise, I found out I was pregnant again. At first the fear crept in about the possibility of losing another pregnancy, but I kept the lake in my mind and just accepted what was to be. My second daughter was born the following spring. As I reflected on the bigger picture, I may or may not have become pregnant again, but I can say with certainty that I would have been at peace with whatever the outcome.

Letting go doesn't mean forgetting about an experience or trying to ignore that it happened. It is about giving yourself an opportunity to acknowledge it, learn from it, and then release it so you can move on without the experience holding you back or getting in the way. It is like a drawing on a chalkboard. We can wipe the board and draw something else, but the dust is still there. It will forever be part of the board, but it doesn't have to rule what else we want to draw in our present moments. It merely adds to the beauty of the image. It creates a depth that cannot be replicated. My letting-go rituals help me honour what has happened and help me accept it. It gives me space to allow for new experiences, new learning, and visits from new everyday mentors.

Chapter Nine

"Huh?"

I think back to that little girl in Grade 5, the one who wanted to be a teacher for kids living with disabilities. Part of me desired to do that because I knew what it felt like to be different. I wanted to comfort them, or just relate and offer hope. It amazes me that I knew, at such a young age, the power of feeling accepted. It feels ironic that I was to have those experiences with my dad, as though I was being tested to look beyond the limitations that others face and then to find ways to connect.

I have struggled as well, living with a disability. Although it isn't as pronounced or obvious as my father's was, it was enough to make me feel different and alone. Very few people know of this, and declaring it is very empowering since I spent many years of my life trying to conceal it.

I am completely deaf in my left ear. I was born without a cochlea, which, of course, is what allows you to hear. This has caused a few anomalies in my appearance such as my left ear being smaller than my right. My left eye is smaller too, and I have vision issues. I talk on one side of my mouth, especially when I am passionate about a topic. A health practitioner once asked me if I had suffered a stroke, because my mouth droops a bit to the side. There is no explanation other than that it is part of who I am. I do not know what stereo sounds like because I have never experienced it. I have had to learn to read lips in order to understand what another person is saying, especially if we are in a loud room. I am afraid of missing something or ignoring someone when I don't mean to. I feared being labelled as a snob for not responding or missing parts of the conversation. Over the years, I have learned to be strategic in where I sit, to hide my disability or at least to not draw attention to it. It has usually worked, except for a few people who discovered my secret when they became perplexed by my insistence on walking on a particular side of them. One woman I worked with some years ago told me I had the most adorable crooked smile. At the time I felt insecure about that observation. Now I am proud of it and am no longer embarrassed and do not feel any less normal because of it. It is part of my unique beauty.

I have many memories of my family lovingly teasing me about my hearing. As a teenager, I would often say "Huh?" when I was asked something. I admit it became an annoying habit, especially around the dinner table. I found myself saying, "Huh?" even if I heard what they had said. One night we saw a TV commercial for a product called Miracle Ear, and this set off a tradition in my house for every time I said, "Huh?" We sang the words Miracle Ear[9] to a similar tune as the Ricola cough candy jingle.[10] It was fun to make light of it and not take myself too seriously. Being deaf in one ear has its benefits, especially at night. Irritating noises, like those of my beloved's snoring or house creaks, are no problem. I just roll over on to my good ear. I have a built-in earplug and off to sleep I go. I have embraced this part of myself and consider it as part of my gift. In a way, I am even grateful for it because it forced me to pay attention and nurture the observer in me.

I believe everyone has a gift—something we were born with that we are meant to express in this world. I also believe we have experiences in life that move us closer to understanding our gift and what we are meant to do in life. Turning inward and reflecting on the wisdom we already carry inside us is enough to get us started in living a fulfilled life in the present.

Taking the time to mentor yourself is the key. You have infinite experiences to draw upon, to reflect on, and invest in. You have all you need inside of you, and the journey will be about finding the resources and support you need in order to uncover them. Your everyday mentors are guiding the way, but it is still up to you to make choices, taking the time to reflect and decide what lessons you want to move forward with. Only you have this power; nobody can do this work for you.

The experiences I have shared throughout this book have led me to an understanding of why I am here. My gift is about being in the moment and being present with myself and others. I embody it fully and it is who I am. What does that mean? I am still figuring that out for myself, but what I do know is that it enables me to be with people, fully and completely. When I am engaged with people, nothing else matters or is happening in my mind. My experiences with my father and my deafness have trained me to be an incredible listener and observer. I would even call myself an expert. This is why I feel I am a gifted coach for others. I have an ability to connect quickly and powerfully if given the opportunity.

I have had thirty-eight years of practice in being inside this unique body. I understand how it works and how to use my disability to enable me to listen and observe closely. What people process with two ears, I have had to do with one, so I became adept at seeing, hearing, and noticing what others may be missing. I also have a great advantage. I can block out noise more easily than most people can. It is not as difficult for me to control how much stimulus my brain is getting because physically there is a block on my left side. I have a natural filter, which is a nice benefit when I feel overwhelmed or if I need to focus on something.

This is why I have a built-in resistance to certain technology and how we connect in our society. We have so many options for how to spend our time and much of the technology today pulls me from being present, going against everything that I am. I cannot be fully present with someone's online profile, so I disengage. I have a hard time being fully present in a large group setting, so I disengage and disappear into the background. I flourish in one-on-one situations and in smaller groups because I can look directly into your eyes. In doing so, I can observe and experience your *being*. I find it difficult to engage in social media for long periods because it depletes me. I desire much more connection than surfing endless updates can provide. If there is too much clutter and noisy background distractions, I find that I cannot be completely present. My nervous system literally starts screaming at me to escape from the crowd. This is why I love coaching. Conversation fills me up, connection fills me up, and being with people and having them share themselves fully feeds my soul. I need a certain level of connection with myself and others in order to access my gift of presence.

So often in life, we allow our thoughts to distract us from being fully in the moment. What extraordinary moments are we missing out on as a result? I admit I cannot be fully present twenty-four hours a day, and I am aware of how my thoughts constantly pull at my attention. My intention is the gradual silencing of not only the external stimuli but also of my internal dialogue. There is so much noise in our world that it is no wonder we constantly feel out of balance. My own journey is about finding my way through the noise and then discovering how to manage it all so I can stay aligned with what matters to me. I want to invest in nurturing my gift rather than nurturing all the distractions.

The discovery of your gift is available to you, possibly right at your fingertips, just as mine was. Ask yourself who the everyday mentors are that pop into your mind and what lessons would they be teaching you in the university lecture hall. These lessons are your road map to your gift, the path to what you are supposed to be nurturing in this life.

I think my dad was my dad for a very specific reason. I needed him and his experience in order for me to understand my own gift and journey. Now that I know who I am and what matters to me, I am excited about life and all its possibilities. The mentors in our lives can be our mirrors, and they can provide us with the building blocks of our foundation. When I became quiet and listened to the messages and the everyday mentors from all around me, my world opened up. My gift of presence is built on the foundation of "Take the time. It is nice to be seen. When it matters, say something." My hearing disability allowed me the opportunity to nurture this gift in a way that someone with full hearing capabilities might not be able to. I am unique and so are you.

And still, I had to be willing to dig deeper. To hold up a mirror, look deeply into my own eyes, and ask myself, "Who do I want to be?"

Part Four

The Lesson Applies Everywhere

Chapter Ten

Hold up Your Mirror

Each lesson we experience and every mentor who crosses our path represents a marker on our journey to becoming whole. Our mentors mirror back to us our greatness and potential. We just need to have the courage to own that greatness and step into it. I was introduced to the concept of mentorship in the corporate world where my role was to build mentorship programs and advise people on how to develop leadership skills. When I look back to the mentorship programs I spearheaded, I feel proud of the part I played and the impact I had on others. The experiences I had in the corporate world and the gift of stepping away from it have shaped my current view of mentorship. I can truly say that I see clearly now.

While I did my best to carve out programs and models that adhered to the parameters and limitations of corporate life, I always felt I had somehow come up short. Taking a step back and looking at the work and my own experiences, what hit me was that I had missed a big piece of the puzzle. I had built a house without a sturdy foundation. No wonder I was feeling I had come up short. I knew I was missing something, but at the time I wasn't able to access what it was until I stepped away from it all.

Wait a minute! I told myself. *You already have the blueprint for transformational mentorship lessons. You have years of experiences filed away in your personal archives.*

In my corporate work, I had been creating programs based on questions like, "What do people need to learn? Who do they need to be paired up with?" I should have been asking, "What do they already know? How do we build from there?"

By not asking those more basic questions, I missed accessing the wealth of wisdom that is buried inside their own and inside all of our unique archives. My focus had been on building the house before setting a strong foundation. If my program was a tree, I now see that I had been starting people up on the trunk rather than digging deep into the seed from which the tree came. It wasn't that people hadn't received value, because it was obvious they had. They told me so. But I think their value would have been tenfold if I had created a program that began with the seed, the foundation, and moved forward from there.

I began to realize that powerful mentorship starts within. I had already experienced the most powerful mentoring relationship. I had been living it with my father. This was where I needed to start, and I invite you to consider where you are starting from as well. I began to look within first, before looking out into the world. Imagine the tree of lessons and knowledge we could create if we took time to discover what made up the seed. I see our experiences and lessons sprouting from the seed, forming roots, growing and expanding. With each experience we have, another beautiful leaf forms and opens. Mentorship for me is about understanding what makes up the seed and then discovering the wisdom of our experiences as it grows. I was surprised at the depth and strength of my wisdom. It was always there, waiting to be discovered. I just had to start exploring.

We take so much time focusing on what we don't know that we miss acknowledging the wisdom in what we already know. We miss paying attention to the growth that brought us to where we are today. Hopefully my story will help you to think about all that you already know. Will it spark a question about all of the people who led you to this knowledge? Will you become an archeologist of your experiences, just as I did? I don't know the answer to that, but what I do know is there is a reason I was called to write these words. I have to at least pose these questions.

I understand that mentorship is a complex and fluid phenomenon. We are continually learning and absorbing information and lessons from others and our environment. It is the classic debate of nature versus nurture. I feel as though I am tapping into that debate a little bit and thus leaving you with the adventure of asking more questions and then wondering. There is always more from which to learn or grow. There will always be wise people who appear in our lives at the right moment to shine a light on what we may need to focus on. One of my core values is a love of learning. I am drawn to anything that expands my view. I love the classroom in whatever form that shows up for me. I have discovered that my depth of learning and my ability to be acutely aware did not flourish until I started looking within. I had to wake up to myself before I could accept the shining light of mentorship all around me. I didn't realize the shining light I was searching for was also shining out of me. I was looking out instead of in. I was surprised at what things I discovered I was already capable of, and you will be as well.

My suggestion is that you begin by looking at the best of your past experiences and lessons. With these as your foundation, you can start building upward and then focus on inviting others to your mentorship party. You can't have a dance without a dance floor. Create your dance floor first and then send out the invitations. I learned the hard way about the results of organizing a (metaphorical) party and sending out the invitations without having the venue booked. I ended up feeling confused and lost. No wonder!

As I mentioned, mentorship is complex. I believe mentorship is defined by the people who have taught, modelled, and shared life lessons. This includes the characteristics we admire in others and the values we carry forward into our own lives. I appreciate that there are mentorship relationships created for us in which we can learn a new skill set. I appreciate that we all have weaknesses and have room to improve. I don't deny that we need other people, classrooms, and workshops to show and share knowledge. I am most curious about the spark inside that moves me toward this love of learning and growing. This spark lives in the core of who I am and is the power source for the spotlight. Perhaps our greatest mentorship experiences have something to do with the lights coming into alignment for each other, or perhaps they are merely beacons that attract us and move us forward. I don't know, but what makes sense to me is that our connection to each other is strong and worth noticing.

For me, mentorship is about addressing who it is that I strive to be and how I process my experiences in order to reflect this. It is characterized by connecting with another person who has walked a path that sparks something inside me, and then taking a moment to reflect on what I am taking away from it. What was important to me about that interaction? Exploration is the path to the growth we seek. I feel I am searching for cues, first to notice when something resonates and then to ask myself "Why?" This is where the possibility of learning lives for me. This is my cue to take a step back and ask myself what I just felt in that moment and why bells are going off. Isn't the basis of mentorship about our own reflection of the experience? There is a spotlight showing us the way, all the time. The power of mentorship relationships is that we can collaborate with someone and guide the spotlight together through sharing. And ultimately, we must understand that where it lands is out of our hands. It just resonates, and our job is to trust it and then do the work to uncover what it all means.

I love the depth of this word *mentorship*. I am merely scratching the surface of its power and all of the possible avenues. I believe at the core of mentorship is connection and the subsequent feeling that something has resonated. I believe you can achieve this connection from one-on-one relationships, and more broadly through storytelling. Books, movies, art, and music, along with all other forms of expression, can be our greatest mentors. Have you ever heard a song for the first time and broke into tears? This is a form of mentorship. The music likely sparked a lesson you hold close, and your values then bubbled to the surface as a reminder of what you stand for. A chance to connect with what matters, what we hold dear, and more importantly, a glimpse into what makes up our foundation. This is one reason I feel compelled to share my story in book form. What if someone resonates with it, learns something about themselves, or sees their circumstances in a different way?

My hunch is that we fail to put ourselves into the mentorship equation as an equal partner. The most powerful thing about mentorship is our perception of our experience. We each have a filter through which we process our experiences. Our observations are powerful because we have infused our own wisdom into them. We have this incredible gift of feeling what the lesson is for each of us. We could both read the same book and I may take away something very different than you will. This is what mentorship means for me. A chance to look within and let your inner knowing guide you to where you need to go next. Look within and trust that exactly what you need to learn from an experience will present itself. This is what will move you forward in life—not someone telling you what you should learn or take away. You have all the answers within you. Your mentorship relationship has to start with you; you will forever feel lost if you seek it in the outside world. Your mentors are the spark and the rest is up to you. How big the fire is and how hot it becomes is really up to you.

As a young leader, I was promoted very early in my career. People would praise me for my leadership skills and ability to connect with people. I always felt like an imposter in accepting the praise because I had very little real work experience as a leader or manager. When I finally asked myself the question, "What do I already know about leading?" I realized that my entire life had been a training course in how to be a leader, which included the great person that others identified me as being. I appreciated the observations because it forced me to wonder how my leadership abilities came about. Well, without even realizing it, all I did was apply the lessons and wisdom—all the stuff my life and especially my experiences with Dad had been presenting to me all along. Our greatest classroom is the one called *life*. Our experiences and life lessons are not something we can post on a résumé. Because they are personal, we need to take the time to discover, uncover, and share what our life has taught us and how it shows up in who we are as employees, friends, and partners. Once we become aware of what makes up our foundation, we will naturally be more powerful. Compare it to growing a garden. If we know where the seeds are, we will water them and they will flourish. Do you know where your seeds are?

Questions I often ask myself are, "What is important to you, Kim? Why is it important?" "What has life taught you about being a leader?" "What special person in your life has impacted your view of what it is to be a leader for others?"

I sometimes think about what my life might be if someone had asked me these questions years ago as a young leader doing her best to navigate what I stood for. What if my managers would have used our one-on-one coffee chats and my career evaluations to ask me these questions instead of simply ticking some vaguely appropriate boxes on a review form? The values that connect me to how I present myself as a leader live in the deep answers to those questions. They live in my being and run through me much in a similar way that my brain remembers to control my breathing without me asking it to. Of course, I can certainly gain more power by mindful breathing. There is power in the conscious awareness of these questions just as there is power in practicing being mindful. I can access my greatness by consciously acknowledging what I stand for and creating more of it in my life. My filters are continually changing, and I am increasingly aware of how powerful my experiences are and how I can use them to guide me in life. All I needed was this awareness. Once I awoke to this, my view of mentorship was never to be the same.

I have been to numerous training programs, listening as keynote speakers encouraged the leaders out there to get to know their people. I realize now that I was trying to provide everyone with all the answers, when the more powerful alternative would have been to ask questions and witness the resulting flow of wisdom. Along the way, I did experience pockets of this flow. It is not my place here to critique the work that I did or didn't do before my personal transformation. I am proud of the connections that I made throughout my time in the corporate world.

I know these realizations are all part of my own growth. What excites me today is the possibility of affecting how people view mentorship in their own lives, whether it is at work or at home. My idea of mentorship is not only about pairing up with an extraordinary person I admire. It's about me, knowing who I am, and then inviting extraordinary people into my world so I can continue to move forward.

If we invest time in answering a few simple questions, the foundation on which we stand will come clearly into our view. I now feel blessed to know who I am and how I show up for myself and for others. This book is about reminding myself to take a bit of time to acknowledge what I learned from my time with Dad and all my mentors for that matter. Because of them and my willingness to dig into what those experiences meant to me, my foundation is set and feels very strong. My journey, as is all of ours in moving forward, is to continue to explore, uncover, and share. We are always mentoring, in every moment. In the midst of every interaction, someone is watching and taking note of who we are and what we have to offer them for their own journey. Mentorship provides the opportunity for us to hold a mirror up and choose the reflection we desire. In turn, our choices give others the opportunity to create the image they wish to see as they hold up their own mirrors. Everyone has a choice in whether to hold up their mirror and seek the answers within.

The reflection in my own mirror is one of awareness. I am becoming more aware, and I especially observe how my choices, my actions, and the language I use impacts what I create and what I focus on. I often notice this while interacting with my kids, who look to me for guidance and meaning. My presence influences the filters they are creating as they process their own experiences. The words I choose hold great power in how they will define themselves and how they perceive the world in the future. It is a great responsibility. I have noticed that conversation about who we hope to be is quite rare. Instead, we teach and are taught how to *do* things—hands-on skills and the like. We ask, "What do you want to *do* when you grow up?" We don't invest much time in conversations such as, "Who are you *being*, and what characteristics matter to you as you learn and interact?" For me, it is more important to be clear on *who you want to be* when doing a job than just solely focusing on doing the job.

With my own kids, when I lose my temper and yell at them, "That's enough. Go to your room!" I am immediately struck with a feeling of "this isn't me" and a knot begins forming in my gut. I feel as though I have been taken over by some other entity for a moment and turned into a monster by the trigger of a child whose reality I struggle to understand and relate to. I notice that I am out of alignment with who I am. So I follow my daughter to her room, take a deep breath, and say, "Honey, I'm sorry for yelling at you. That is not the mom I want to be. I don't like to yell—it feels yucky. I want to be a calm, caring mom for you."

"Okay, Mom. I'm sorry too. I love you," she chirps.

My hope is to show her and share with her who I want to be for her as she grows up, especially at times when I feel that I falter in my parenting. It is important to me to keep conversations open and to take a step back when I notice that an interaction didn't feel just right. I can always grow and be the best version of myself but it takes knowing what matters to me and what I want to nurture. It takes awareness and a commitment to get back on track.

I notice this most often when people have conversations with kids about the future. We always seem to automatically ask the same type of question we were asked: "What do you want to *do* when you grow up?"

"When I grow up I want to be a teacher," I remember proudly declaring.

But the *be* is usually referring to *doing* something as a profession and not who I will *be* while teaching. I think we owe it to our children to keep asking more questions. Let's dig a little deeper for their sakes. For example, a little boy shares that he wants to be a firefighter when he grows up. I want to know what type of person that boy wants to be while he is fighting the fires. Will he be known for being the friendly, loyal, hardworking, honest, joyful firefighter? Or will he be known for being a miserable, arrogant, bullying, power-hungry firefighter?

What is it about being a firefighter that inspired this little boy in the first place? Has he seen firefighters in action, whether in real life or in the movies, and something was sparked inside him? This is what I would like to know, and I suspect it has more to do with *being* than wearing a cool uniform. What if we all committed to asking two more questions? What would the little boy take away from this interaction if we asked a few more questions?

I often wonder why we invest more time on what we plan on *doing* in life than on who we plan on *being* in our life. Why is it that we don't teach people how to process the experiences they have had?

We don't teach people to take the time to reflect on their learnings. We don't teach people about the power of asking themselves the deeper kinds of questions about what matters and why it matters. We don't teach people about what it means to feel worthy and enough inside.

There is a good side to all of this. We are evolving, and the values we hold close are increasingly being shared as community values. I am excited about the conversations I will have with my kids compared with the conversations my great-grandma had with her parents. A shift is happening and I hope to honour my ancestors by being a big part of this shift.

Imagine what conversations we might have if we had a *being* course in our schools and universities, where people could dig into who they are and who helped shape them. Imagine the dinner table conversations at home. Imagine the young adults we would be sending out into the world if they knew themselves at much deeper levels. Imagine if we talked about what we took away from an experience. What lessons affected us at the level of our soul, and why?

How would this influence their choice of a career, a life partner? How would it affect just making everyday decisions that shape all parts of their lives? How would this influence the words they choose to use in conversation? What if each person, before making a move, asked himself or herself, "Am I being who I want to be in this situation?"

This is how I now live my life and I am happier for it. I do wonder what the impact of the above would be, one reader at a time. The possibility of this kind of conversation inspires me, and I am excited about being part of this possibility as a coach. If even one person, by reading this book, decides to look in the mirror and a twinkle of curiosity sparks them into discovering themselves at a deeper level, then that is my measure of success. What do you want to see in the mirror? Hold it up and ask—"Who do I want to be?"

Chapter Eleven

Check Yourself

My hope is that you see my story as more than just some chapters about someone who has moved through a tough experience. My hope is that you will see how powerful many of your own experiences are. I encourage everyone to share your greatest lessons as a way to develop more capability in your work lives, regardless of how big or how small your work teams are. What if your mentorship programs started with a model of knowing yourself first? What if you celebrated your life lessons rather than burying them as you walk through the door where you work? Early in my career, often from my own leaders, I heard phrases such as "Check your baggage at the door" or "Check yourself at the door." Time to go on stage and put on a smile. I noticed that what they intended to say and what I heard were two very different things.

As I heard chatter in the lunchroom and observed behaviours of my team, I began to wonder what they internalized this catch phrase to mean.

"Don't be myself." "My experiences and wisdom don't matter." "I need to be a robot for the customers." "Don't let on I am struggling or having a tough day. Push it way down." "Fit into the cookie-cutter mould."

The intention of "checking your baggage at the door" clearly meant that you were to do your best to let go of anything that might get in the way of you being fully present for your job responsibilities. However, without context, catchy phrases can be dangerous in the workplace. But I also think they can serve as a great opportunity to open up conversations that normally might not happen. It is too bad that this doesn't happen, since most of us don't take the time to unpack the meaning of what is presented.

    I don't disagree that we need to shake off what we are holding on to and be present when we are out in the world. I agree that employees need to check in with themselves and ask, "What do I need right now in order to be at my best?" What was missing for me in this message was acknowledging that we all have baggage and then encouraging us to honour our experiences rather than stuffing them. As I reflect on my own journey, especially in my work, I recall that I expended a lot of energy covering up what was going on inside. I became an expert at checking myself at the door and putting on a smile as I walked through the sliding doors into work. It took a lot out of me, and I was often not authentic. I did everything in my power to please and be the employee that I thought they wanted. The falseness of it all built up to the point where it blew up.

    The day with my dad in the kitchen, when he said, "I can't see," was my starting point for bottling up my emotions. All was calm on the surface, but the heat of the lava was bubbling and bubbling. It took many years, but the tipping point eventually came. A situation at work with my boss spiralled out of control due to a miscommunication, and when he called me out during a team meeting, I couldn't hold it in any longer. I exploded. I sobbed uncontrollably, feeling powerless. There I was, at the boardroom table, head down in shame, trying desperately to hide my explosion of tears. I was completely paralyzed by my emotions, and worse, I felt humiliated that I was losing control in front of my peers. I excused myself and went to the bathroom where I hyperventilated for thirty minutes, sobbing. I couldn't stop. I became angry with myself, I prayed, and none of it worked for me to regain control. I just sobbed. It was all coming out. I had finally lost the control I had so desperately sought to maintain for so long. Here I was, someone who prided herself as being a successful young leader, responsible for a team of people, now sitting on top of a toilet seat, releasing every painful moment I had stuffed away for the last twelve years. This was a defining experience—a mentoring experience that shaped how I presented myself as a leader since then. I no longer asked anyone to check themselves at the door. My style of leadership completely altered after that day: I accepted that we have the right to show up just as we are, feeling just as we do. I allowed my people to move through their experiences in whichever way they needed to. When I noticed inauthentic smiles, I began to ask questions rather than just walk by. I made up my mind that I wanted to connect, see people, and take time to be with them wherever they were in their own journey.

I think this event started me on a path of acceptance. I was twenty-six years old, and I no longer wanted to stuff my feelings about my life. I wanted to live into my name. I wanted to be a person who could "stand even" despite all the heartache. I wanted to use my experiences to inspire me rather than have them drag me down. I knew there was much more to discover, but this incident was the beginning of letting it out and asking for what I needed. It was the point where I realized bottling my feelings up was no longer working, and as the years passed it grew stronger and stronger, while the walls I had once built became weaker and weaker.

I think we are tested all the time. As I began writing this book, I had someone say to me that I shouldn't write about both my dad and mentorship in the same book. They advised me to write a memoir and then perhaps write about mentorship in a separate format. For them and their perspective on life, it didn't make sense to tie the two together. I suddenly had that "check your baggage at the door" feeling, and although I respected the person's opinion, I had to disagree and continue to write this book from an authentic place. My mentorship wisdom occurred because of my personal experiences. I had to choose to stay true to my vision, regardless of the opinions out there in the world. I think the corporate world might benefit greatly from exploring what they really expect from their employees and life itself. We aren't robots or numbers. Without this exploration, people are going to shrivel, doing their best to dismiss their own legitimate experiences and focus on what others want them to be or learn. Maybe this is why we experience so many eruptions in our workplace, so many interpersonal conflicts and miscommunications. I wonder if it is because we are not acknowledging the fact that many of us are becoming walking volcanos. Asking more questions and creating a culture of curiosity, caring, and compassion may diffuse some of these imminent explosions.

The "put on a smile" model isn't working anymore. Employees can't sustain "checking their baggage at the door" any longer. There is a hunger to add something more meaningful to our time at work than just acting robotic. What I am suggesting is access for people to begin feeling *more* in their lives. It is time that we embrace all of who we are, both at work and at home. That is why I wrote a book placing my dad and a mentorship philosophy inside the same cover. I want to invite you and everyone to access the wisdom from your everyday mentors so you can be the best of yourself in whatever role in which you find yourself.

I would like to invite leaders and those who are currently in formal mentoring positions to stop long enough to consider introducing a conversation about what their protégés know and believe. Besides reading what they have placed in their résumés, ask people about what life itself has taught them. It all matters. There is so much more to discover about the people with whom we interact. Along with many others, I am sure, I have grown weary of trying to compartmentalize my life experiences into:

- those that are appropriate for work,
- those that are appropriate for my personal life,
- those that are appropriate for these friends, and
- those that are appropriate for family.

Trying to filter experiences, while picking what I can and can't be open about, is exhausting. I believe the process that works best for me is to trust myself in the moment and share authentically when it feels right. I am not going to hide and try to fit in by disappearing. Been there, done that. This is where the "If it matters, say something," really resonates for me. Check *in* with yourself rather than checking *out*. Check in and ask yourself the questions, "How important is this to me?" "What do I stand for?"

What if we were to examine ourselves and one another from a holistic perspective? What if everyone took a moment to reflect on what their life has already offered them and how those things can serve them in all other areas of their life? I am not suggesting that you should send out a company-wide memo declaring all of your life lessons. It can be a subtle kind of sharing with a trusted leader in one-on-one conversations. Or merely just asking yourself the question and reflecting on it. My point is that I experienced a special journey full of lessons with my dad and then went to work, carrying with me what was in the lessons. I had breakups, amazing travel experiences, a wedding, two miscarriages, two children, the death of loved ones, and a cancer scare. I also lived through the ups and downs of chronic pain and hearing loss and still had to show up at work. I still had to show up in life and carry on. But I no longer wanted to check any of it at the door, at any door. Instead, I gradually learned to bring it all with me and use it in a mindful, positive way. Ultimately, the learning in all of life's vicissitudes is more about how I react to things rather than about the events themselves.

This is what Dad taught me. I can use the lessons of "Take the time. It's nice to be seen. When it matters, say something" with my clients, my kids, my husband, my teammates—with everyone. These lessons are relevant for all experiences. Your lessons are as relevant to you as mine are for me. As I accumulate more experiences, I know I can continue to find the core lessons that will help me in becoming who I strive to be.

We don't have to check our baggage or ourselves at the door. We can be inspired by our experiences, whether they are tragic or uplifting, and use them to create something. They can help us move forward and help us to be the best of ourselves.

Imagine for a moment if everyone on your team, in your family, and in your circle of friends, used their life lessons to their full advantage. What if they took the time to become aware and discovered how these life lessons had been moving them closer to discovering their life's purpose? What if this awareness propelled them and motivated them in every part of their work and in their lives in general? What if families and organizations created an environment where people felt safe to share what they have learned and what inspires them?

I understand why, to some, it may seem odd that I have combined my father's story with a mentorship message. I understand why someone might think, "Why would you be sharing something so personal and linking it to something that may involve the workplace?" The answer? It's because it is who I am. I cannot do one without the other. I cannot work with a client without accessing the lessons I learned from my journey with my dad. Without me telling my story, you might have had an interaction with me and not know that I was accessing lessons from my early personal experiences—unless I had told you at some point. You need not write your own book or declare your deepest experiences on stage at a work conference or at the dinner table. But it is worth considering for a few moments what lessons resonate for you from your everyday mentors and how this perspective could transform your life. What if we all put our greatest lessons into action every day? What would the impact be?

This book is about opening up possibilities as a result of our life lessons. It is about being mindful, taking the time to access the wisdom you have deep within you, and sharing that wisdom in your daily actions. I want to be part of a world where we are encouraged to be our authentic selves at work and at home. I want to be part of a world that supports the idea that we do not have to separate our work lives from our personal lives. We can check in with ourselves and decide in the moment what we want to put out there. We do not have to check out or deny our experiences to satisfy someone else's agenda. We can be whole, anywhere, everywhere. We can be inspired by our whole life.

Chapter Twelve

Be Inspired

I had no idea of the depth of grief until I had to climb out of it. I can speak only from my own experience dealing with tragedy, but what I know is that it is easy to become trapped. I was engulfed in the numbness, and it was only when I gave myself permission to experience the emotions of grief fully that I started to live again. Grief is part of being human and is something that can connect us and that we can all relate to. I feel it is my turn to mentor others through their experiences. My dad passed the torch to me. I feel I have a responsibility to the world to "stand even" and shout out loud that with unimaginable grief comes immeasurable inspiration. Because it matters. You have to make a choice to take the time to uncover your unique gift, see it in yourself, and be willing to use it. The only mentor you need right now is yourself. Yes, you will learn amazing and meaningful lessons from others, but you are missing a huge piece of the puzzle if you don't first start with yourself. The insights from others will be richer if you first do the work to uncover your foundation. Pick the lessons that drive the behaviour you wish to create in yourself, and let go of the ones that don't align with what you want to create. Once you connect with the amazing lessons inside yourself, other people will appear in your life to shine a light and help you deepen what you need to see and learn. I learned that the death of someone I love is not a death sentence for me. My loved ones are the ones who died, not me. I don't have to die along with them; they wouldn't want that. They whisper in my ear to live and be inspired by the fact that I shared experiences with them. I give myself permission to be sad, to be angry if it is necessary, and to experience whatever emotion is present. Then I ask myself, "What's next? What inspired me about this experience?" This is how I was able to move forward in a healthy, balanced way.

When I think about my dad, I do not think about the fact that I wasn't there when he took his last breath. I don't think about the moment of his death. I choose to remember the amazing memories that bring tears of joy to my eyes when I think of him. I have a picture of him with his two Harley Davidson motorcycles. I remember going for a ride with him around our community when I was a young teenager. *Check this out. My dad is the coolest.* I would think, as people watched us ride by. Holding on to him and feeling the freedom of riding, I had a glimpse of why he loved it so much. I think about that day whenever I ride my quad across our vast fields. He joins me in my thoughts.

I remember to laugh. My dad's girlfriend told a story during one of my visits to their house. He was fortunate to be able to stay in his own home for twelve years under her care. Most nights, our large golden retriever, Bailey, slept in bed with Dad. One night they became all tangled up to the point where Bailey's legs were up the back of Dad's underwear and all they could do was lie there, waiting to be rescued. Our family has shared this story countless times, and it still makes me laugh as if I am hearing it the first time. I think about that day. I want to feel inspired when I think about my dad and his life. I am not saying that I don't feel sad sometimes. Yes, I do, but what I've been noticing is that it doesn't last as long. I am training myself to shift into happy memories when he pops into my mind. That is how I want to honour his life, rather than to have it be about a few painful moments.

I've found that the key to moving through grief is to create. Create something in honour of the person or persons. Live life fully in their honour; experience something they would have loved to experience, knowing that they are with you in spirit. Their story mattered, so do something with it. Make it part of your own legacy so it lives on. My kids know Grandpa Ed even though he isn't here in body. They know him, and he will be part of their lives because I am inspired to re-create my experiences with Dad for them through the stories I tell them.

Be inspired by death because it is going to happen to all of us. We can't control it or change it. Pretending that reality doesn't exist does not mean it isn't there. So embrace it, accept it, and use it to create your life. Don't shut it down because it is uncomfortable. Embrace all the ways death shows up in our lives. A person's final breath is just one part of it. We have endings and beginnings all the time.

My grief about Dad began in that kitchen long ago, the moment he started to have bleeding in his brain. It started the moment I heard, "I can't see." That was the death of my current reality. Life as I knew it had now died. People die, pets die, experiences and chapters in our lives die, and we are left with memories and lessons. Be inspired by what you are left with. Be inspired by the new beginning. Be inspired about the lessons you were gifted with. We are all mentors and mentees, and absorbing and sharing lessons has to start with us.

If you are open to the possibility that your lessons can provide you with new ways of living, then that is all you need. That is the mentorship model I want to leave you with. It is the first step in creating awareness, a new perspective, and a new way of living. It is all in you and up to you. The responsibility is yours, so choose to take the time to uncover and declare your intentions for yourself. You do not need anyone else. You do not need an executive mentor to help you start this journey. Start with yourself first and the mentors you need will appear beside you when you need them. This is what happened to me. When I started writing this book, the people I needed to make it the best it could be just presented themselves because I had done the work. I have uncovered my foundation, and the mentors I need to move forward to deepen my learning are presenting themselves even as I write this. I trust they will continue to do so as I keep walking my path.

And now on to opening the next door …

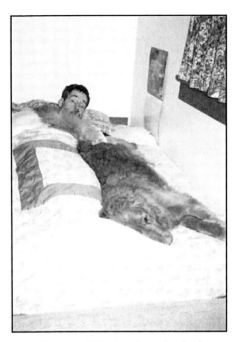

Dad and Bailey shared a bed.

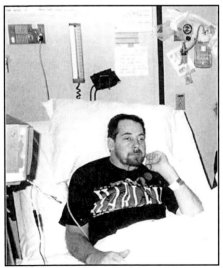

The hospital room—many months of recovery.

Dad, a few short years before his first brain bleed.

Afterword

Take Action and Share Yourself

Are you inspired by what you have discovered so far? Take action and share. Join the Mentor Message Movement.

www.facebook.com/mentormessage

If you have a mentor in your life who has changed how you view the world, I would love to hear from you.

Who would you place on your wall of history, and how have they lit the path for your own growth and learning?

Send me a postcard or an email describing who your mentor was/is and the message that shifted your life. I will post all the messages on Facebook and my website. I believe we can change how we all see the world by sharing about the people who touch our souls. We can be better, and I feel it is my mission to create a space for our collective growth. I am offering you a place to share so you can access what you need. Take the time, create a message, and send it today.

Mail:

Mentor Messages
Box 89
Mariapolis, MB
R0K 1K0

Email:

mentormessage@gmail.com

You can find more information at:

www.kimstandeven.com/mentormessage

Do Better

Journal Activity

"When you know better, you do better." —Maya Angelou[11]

This quote rings in my ear. I hear my mother's voice since she says it all the time.

There are many messages you can take away from reading this book. I am not going to suggest to you what they are. It's up to you to decide what it is that you need at this moment. For me, everything that I am is about being a better version of myself than I was yesterday. Picking myself up when I crumble and trying again. I mentioned my dream of the possibility of more focused *being* conversations in our classrooms, boardrooms, and around our dinner tables. My hope is that reading this inspires you to be and do better, and to start those conversations.

As leaders in our workplaces and our homes, my hope is that we spend more time reflecting on the environment we are creating. What kind of playground are you creating? One of fear, shame, and hiding what matters to you, as I felt in Grade 5? Or one of curiosity, learning, and sharing? One of authenticity, acceptance, and inquiry? I believe that the only way we will "know better" is by taking the time to uncover what makes up our foundation. Honouring our everyday mentors is a way to access knowing better. It will naturally lead to being and doing better in our relationships with our loved ones and in our roles at work. It just takes a willingness to be open to the messages and the taps on the shoulder when they come. By doing the work, your life will be transformed in ways beyond your imagination.

I am proof of that. My perspective has expanded, and I feel as if I have finally broken free from the weight of those experiences I was entangled in. I feel like a butterfly that has finally broken free from its cocoon. I believe everyone wants to be free from the chains of fear and pain. It *is* possible—through sharing, exploring, and mentoring.

It can start right here, right now with some journal activity. Through writing in a journal, you can mentor yourself and start on the journey of transformation.

In the following pages are the questions I used as I explored the messages that came that early morning. I gift them to you as you start on your own mentorship journey.

Your Space

It is crucial for you to create a space that nurtures reflection. This is not an exercise you can do while distracted.

Create a space that is silent, calm, and where you feel the most comfortable without the temptation of technology or other people.

Your Space Journal Question:

Where is the best space or place where you can get quiet, feel relaxed, and have time to reflect?

For me, it first happened at 3:00 a.m. I was alone and able to write, uninterrupted and without judgement, until no more words came and I could return to sleep. I have since created a room in my home that is my own, my quiet place. It is a place where all my favourite books and images are. It is a place in which I can sit and enjoy the silence and just be. There is no technology in this room, just a window, a chair, a chalkboard, and a desk.

I asked one of my clients one day, "What is your favourite thing in nature?" She said, "Moss." After some conversation, we were talking about her needing to access some answers and she said, "I need to be with the moss." She needed to be in a mossy forest to access answers to questions she has. There is no right or wrong answer about which space you need to achieve serenity; all that matters is that you connect to it. Answering this first question is a glimpse into uncovering your own wisdom. One question at a time. Trust yourself.

Everyday Mentors

Close your eyes and imagine you are at a café waiting for an invited guest. You notice the door swing open and the face of your everyday mentor comes into view. They sit with you and share a warm comforting drink and you share memories.

Everyday Mentor Journal Question:

What memories stand out when you think about your mentor?

When you ask for guidance, it will almost always present itself in some form. You just have to be aware and notice.

Dig Deeper

Once you have selected some key experiences, ask yourself the following questions. Write spontaneously what comes to mind, with no editing.

> ### Dig Deeper Journal Question:
> What values or lessons are present in those cherished memories?
>
>
>
> Does a statement emerge that might capture the essence of the lesson?

Dig Even Deeper

Reread what you wrote. Ask yourself more questions. Give yourself permission to take the time.

Dig Even Deeper Journal Question:

What statements or words are
jumping off the page at you?

Now imagine you are sitting in a university lecture hall.

What is the lecture about?

What are you hearing?

Write freely again. When you are finished, congratulations! You have just mentored yourself.

Complete this process until you feel you have a solid foundation in which to explore further.

This is what I did with the messages from my dad. As I have mentioned, my foundation is "Take time. It's nice to be seen. And when it matters, say something."

Within these three statements, I ultimately uncovered all of the values that I hold dear and that drive my behaviour. Now I can focus on attracting new mentors into my life to help shine a light on deepening these values and learning more about myself.

Unlock the wisdom within

If you are serious about ...

- Discovering the lesson in your most memorable experiences
- Unlocking what matters to you and why
- Being the best version of yourself

Then visit

WWW.KIMSTANDEVEN.COM/MENTORMESSAGE

Where you can register for a complimentary 45 minute *'Unlock your Mentorship Wisdom'* strategy session.

During this 45 minutes, I will help you to:

- Articulate your greatest mentorship lessons
- Identify the building blocks of your foundation
- Create a clear vision of how to put the lessons into practice

It started with me. And it starts with you.

Mentorship Model

A Look Within

Mentorship Model—All Rights Reserved 2016

Wisdom

Wisdom sits solidly in the middle of this model, providing your foundation. It is continuously being fed by your experiences, your values, your investment in exploration, and your expanding view as you move through life. Your foundation may shift and deepen based on how much exploration you invest in and to what degree you expand your perspectives.

Experience—In every experience there is a lesson and a test of your values.

What do you already know based on the experiences you have had? Who are the people who showed you the way? What did they teach you?

Exploration—Deepen your understanding, explore meaning, and reflect on what you have discovered.

Why are the lessons in your foundation important to you? What matters about what you have discovered? What you choose to explore will shift based on your discoveries.

Expansion—New perspectives, moments of clarity, and increased inspiration.

What is possible based on what you have discovered? What do you want to create more of? What actions do you want to take? What's next for you? What are you curious about? What additional learning do you feel you need?

How you expand will depend on your foundation and your investment in exploration. This is also the space where new mentorship relationships present themselves. The learning from here will continue to feed your foundation and your desire to explore.

Experience, exploration, and expansion are all connected. As one grows, so will the others, and this is where your mentorship journey starts. The model flows just like the dance of life, and it is up to you to decide when to dance, when to rest, and when to reflect.

Acknowledgments

This book is more than just me. There is a lifetime of experiences and others who are connected to what I have learned. My words are not my own entirely. I have been influenced by so many wonderful mentors, those whom I know personally and those who are out in the world sharing their voices and wisdom. Everyone I have encountered is in here in some way, and I thank you.

To my mom, Penny. You showed me what determination looks like. Without your perseverance and tenacity with your own health journey, I would never have had the courage to reach for my dreams. You inspire me!

To my husband, Joedy. Thank you for accepting me as I am and loving me as you do. Thank you for not giving up on me when life gets hard and for making me laugh. I love you very much.

To Dan, Natasha, Rachel, Heidi, and Larry. You have seen me at my best and at my worst. We have grown up together and I thank you for loving me despite my quirks and mistakes. I look forward to our future laughs.

To Lori Anne, Terra, and Liz. Each of you catapulted me into my journey to finding my voice. You transformed my life and showed me how. I am inspired by our connection and our continued learning. I am awake because of each of you. I am awake because of *Authentic to the Core* and coaching. No words can express my gratitude.

To Lori-Anne Demers. Thank you for your guidance, mentorship, and for writing the beautiful forward to this book. WWW.DEMERSGROUP.COM

To Laurel, my cheerleader. This book would not have been written without your words of encouragement. You believed in me when I didn't believe in myself.

To Rich Orlesky. You are an incredible writer, mentor and friend. Without your guidance, editing and feedback, this book would not be what it is. I am forever grateful for your wisdom and support. WWW.RICHMATTERS.COM

To Arlene Prunkl. Thank you for your exquisite editing and feedback. WWW.PENULTIMATEWORD.COM

To Kate and Alexandra, my greatest mentors. You inspire me to be and do better every day.

To all of the amazing women in my life. You give me hope and strength.

To my clients. Thank you for trusting me with your deepest thoughts, dreams, and desires. I am moved by each of our conversations and I am in awe of your incredible wisdom.

To all the caregivers who give selflessly of their time and energy to care for loved ones who are living with disabilities or illness. I understand the struggles you face and I honour your commitment.

Endnotes

[1] Caged Bird Legacy LLC website: Continuing the life work of Maya Angelou. http://mayaangelou.com/ (2016). Accessed 11 July 2016.

[2] Adele, song "Million Years Ago," from the album *25*, XL Recordings (2015).

[3] *Happy Days*, TV series, produced by Gary Marshall, ABC Television (1974).

[4] Simon and Garfunkel, song "I Am a Rock," from the album *Simon and Garfunkel's Greatest Hits*, CBS Inc. (1982).

[5] Energizer Bunny TV commercial, introduced 1989, Eveready Battery Co. Inc. YouTube, TV Rewind. https://www.youtube.com/watch?v=fILdYrxnrf8. Accessed 11 July 2016.

[6] *Uncle Buck*, film, directed by John Hughes, Universal Studios (1989).

[7] *Trains, Planes and Automobiles*, film, directed by John Hughes, Paramount Pictures (1987).

[8] Workshop: Authentic to the Core, Banff, Canada. Creator L.A. Demers (March, 2012), www.demersgroup.com.

[9] Miracle Ear TV commercial, introduced 1987. YouTube, Video Archeology (2012). https://www.youtube.com/watch?v=4IJwJ9Xlj-c. Accessed 11 July 2016.

[10] Ricola TV commercial, aired 2011–2013. YouTube, Philippe Vonlanthen (2011). https://www.youtube.com/watch?v=4Q5IA2Epk9Y. Accessed 11 July 2016.

[11] Caged Bird Legacy LLC website: Continuing the life work of Maya Angelou. http://mayaangelou.com/. Accessed 11 July 2016.

About the Author

I used to pray that I wouldn't cry. I remember the first time vividly a few weeks after hearing the news my parents were getting a divorce. Along with my brother, I was riding my bike to Dad's house to see him. It was the first time since hearing the news, and I prayed, riding down the long hill, to the wind in my face to dry my tears. I prayed that I wouldn't cry. It wasn't that I didn't want to cry for myself; it was the fact that I didn't want my dad to see my pain. I wanted to protect him from additional heartache. I succeeded. My brother and I walked in the door, and the first thing Dad did was cry. This was the first time I had ever seen him upset. He cried and frantically tried to make a cup of coffee to distract himself. I held it back the entire time. *Please don't cry. Please don't cry.* I didn't.

As I look back on that moment, I wish I had let myself cry. Blocking it created more damage than I ever could have imagined and a hell of a lot more work in learning to feel. At the age of thirty-three, I decided that I would never hold back my tears ever again. I promised my ten-year-old self that I would honour my feelings and cry as little or as much as I needed in the moment. It is funny—at the workshop where I learned to let go, one of the participants shared with the group that the one thing they appreciated about me was that I cried so openly without shame. She said that by doing so I gave her permission to show emotion as well. That meant a lot to me, and I will continue to shed as many tears as it takes to create the space for others to do so as well. I will never pray away my tears again. Never.

I am an open book. If you ask me a question, I will answer you authentically. I have nothing to hide, and my life is about accessing what matters to me, trusting myself, and sharing. This is who I choose to be. I am a teacher, healer, author, coach, mentor, mother, wife, sister, daughter, friend, and spiritual being put here to share and create.

Career Bio

I have over a decade of leadership experience in the aviation field combined with professional coaching certification, a bachelor of psychology degree, and a certificate in human resource management to support employees in organizations to live balanced, fulfilled, and purposeful lives. Today, I run my own coaching business. My passion and purpose is to partner with people to empower them to create a life that is aligned with their true selves. Through powerful conversations, training, and personal development workshops, I have witnessed people transform their careers, relationships, and self-worth. My compassionate, open, and supportive style creates an environment for my clients to succeed. I have experienced much success in supporting my clients in making positive changes in their lives and careers.

International Coaching Federation Associate Certified Coach (ACC)
Licenced Interpersonal Wellness System Facilitator
Licenced Authentic to the Core facilitator

Kim Standeven ACC, BA
CORE ALIGNMENT COACH

---

kimstandeven.com
facebook.com/kimstandevencoach
facebook.com/mentormessage

Live Life with Ease and Grace

If you are ready to ...

- Let go of past experiences that are weighing you down
- Effectively manage stress
- Trust your decision making
- Expand your creativity and personal expression
- Discover your Life's Purpose

Then attend the

Authentic to the Core Workshop

Join Kim Standeven for this 3-day retreat and discover what it means to live life from the core of who you are.

For more information and registration details, visit www.kimstandeven.com/workshops-events

Be one of the thousands of people who have awakened to themselves by attending this workshop. For over 20 years, this workshop has been offered as a public retreat, in organizations, and as a continuing education course.

Grab your seat today and transform your life by:
Remembering who you are
Discovering what you love
Being true to yourself

Did you know...

Less than 1% of the general population or 1 in 100,000 people will experience a brain AVM (Arteriovenous Malformation).
- AVMs are a tangle of abnormal and poorly formed blood vessels (arteries and veins).
- AVMs can occur anywhere in the body. Brain AVMs are of special concern because of the damage they cause when they bleed.

http://brainavm.uhnres.utoronto.ca/malformations/brain_avm_index.htm

28% of Canadians aged 15 and older provide care to family members or friends with long-term health conditions, disability needs, or aging needs. (2013 Statistics Canada)

http://www.statcan.gc.ca/daily-quotidien/130910/dq130910a-eng.htm

Nearly half of Canadians (13 million) have provided care to a family member or friend at some point (2016 report).

http://vanierinstitute.ca/wp-content/uploads/2016/02/2016-02-22_Family-caregiving-in-Canada.pdf

13.7% of Canadians aged 15 years and older reported some type of disability, and among them, 7.2% of Canadian adults were identified as having a mobility disability that limited their daily activities (2012 Statistics Canada).

http://www.statcan.gc.ca/pub/89-654-x/89-654-x2016005-eng.htm

I am certain that all of us will face a challenge whether caused by aging, disease, or accident. My father may have been in the 1% with his particular diagnosis, but I know there are millions of us out there struggling to make sense of the challenges we are facing. I don't have the answer to why, but I do know that together we can get through it. Together, we can survive and face another day knowing that we are connected to what matters to us most.

Twenty-five years ago, our family didn't have access to the support there is today. Whatever you may be dealing with in life, there is support. Together we can heal, together we can persevere.

Ask for help—please don't suffer in silence. You are not alone.

Kim Standeven
CORE ALIGNMENT COACH

About Kim Standeven Core Alignment Coaching Services

Kim Standeven partners with individual clients, families, and organizations to improve overall wellness at work and at home with an emphasis on:

- Leadership
- Communication
- Work/Life Balance
- Goal Setting
- Value Discovery
- Wellness Assessments

Kim Standeven offers one-on-one coaching, group and team coaching, customized workshops, and speaking. Kim is available for interviews, retreats, and events.

For more information, please visit
www.kimstandeven.com
www.facebook.com/kimstandevencoach
www.facebook.com/mentormessage

Join the Mentor Message Movement

www.facebook.com/mentormessage
www.kimstandeven.com/mentormessage

"Stand Even, No Matter What Happens in Life"
—Kim Standeven

Thank you for supporting my dream.

Reflect on your greatest mentorship lesson. Cut out the postcard, create your message on the back, and mail it. When we reflect and share, we grow.

Mentor Message

Box 89
Mariapolis, MB
R0K 1K0
Canada

www.facebook.com/mentormessage
@mentormessage

Who do you want to honor? What life lesson do you want to share?
Get creative on the back and mail.

We are gifted with wisdom. Let's honor our mentors and share it.

Stamp goes here